# OF LOVE
# AND DUST

———

# OF LOVE
# AND DUST

*by* ERNEST J. GAINES

W. W. NORTON & COMPANY
NEW YORK · LONDON

This book is dedicated to
LeVell Holmes
and
Alice Ryan Holmes

W. W. Norton & Company, Inc., 500 Fifth Avenue,
New York, N.Y. 10110

W. W. Norton & Company, Inc., also publishes *The Norton Anthology of English Literature*, edited by M. H. Abrams et al; *The Norton Anthology of Poetry*, edited by Arthur M. Eastman et al; *World Masterpieces*, edited by Maynard Mack et al; *The Norton Reader*, edited by Arthur M. Eastman et al; *The Norton Facsimile of the First Folio of Shakespeare*, prepared by Charlton Hinman; *The Norton Anthology of Modern Poetry*, edited by Richard Ellmann and Robert O'Clair; *The Norton Anthology of Short Fiction*, edited by R. V. Cassill; *The Norton Anthology of American Literature*, edited by Ronald Gottesman et al; and the *Norton Critical Editions*.

**Library of Congress Cataloging in Publication Data**

Gaines, Ernest J        1933–
Of love and dust.

I. Title.
PZ4.G14220f 1979 [PS3557.A355]   813'.5'4   78-26032
ISBN 0-393-00914-9

3 4 5 6 7 8 9 0

# PART ONE

# 1
_____

From my gallery I could see that dust coming down the
quarter, coming fast, and I thought to myself, "Who in the
world would be driving like that?" I got up to go inside
until the dust had all settled. But I had just stepped inside
the room when I heard the truck stopping before the gate.
I didn't turn around then because I knew the dust was flying
all over the place. A minute or so later, when I figured it
had settled, I went back. The dust was still flying across the
yard, but it wasn't nearly as thick now. I looked toward the
road and I saw somebody coming in the gate. It was too dark
to tell if he was white or colored.

"You Kelly?" he said, when he came up to the steps.

He was a tall, slim, brown-skin boy. He had on a dirty,
light-color shirt and dark pants. The collar of his shirt was
unbuttoned and the sleeves were rolled up to the elbows.

"I'm Kelly," I said. "Jim Kelly."

"He want you out there," the boy said, nodding toward
the gate. "Mind if I have some water?"

"Some in the icebox in the kitchen."

He came up the steps to go by me, and I could see how
he was sweating and I could smell the sweat in his clothes.
I went out to the truck where Sidney Bonbon was sitting

behind the steering wheel. Bonbon was the overseer of the plantation. He still had on that sweat-stained white straw hat and he was still wearing the dirty, sweat-smelling khakis he had worn in the field that day. He was looking at Charlie Jordan's old house on the other side of the road. Charlie had his light on in the front room, and he and somebody else were sitting out on the gallery.

"Yeah?" I said leaning on the truck.

Bonbon turned to me.

"Doing anything?" he said.

"Sitting down."

"Take him to Baton Rouge. Get his clothes and bring him on back here. He got that room 'side you there."

I wanted him to tell me more about the boy.

"Anything in there?" he asked.

"A stove; no pipe," I said. "That's about all."

"No bed?"

"No; they had an old cot in there, but somebody must have taken it."

"If he don't get one in Baton Rouge, they got one in the tool shop," Bonbon said. "He get the rest from the store."

I nodded my head. I still wanted to know more about the boy. Who was he? What was he doing there?

"I'm putting him there 'side you; he be working with you from now on," Bonbon said. "Jonas going in the cotton field."

The boy came back and stood by the truck.

"You ready?" Bonbon said to me.

"I'm ready," I said. I turned to the boy. "You shut the door?"

"I closed it."

"Hop in," I said.

He got in the middle and I got in beside him. It was blaz-

4

ing hot in there with all three of us crammed together. Bonbon went down the quarter to turn around at the railroad tracks, then he shot back up the quarter just as fast as he had come down there. I knew what to expect when he came up to his house, so I braced myself. The boy didn't know what was coming, and when Bonbon slammed on brakes, the boy struck his forehead against the dashboard.

"Goddamn," he said.

"All right, Geam," Bonbon said to me. He acted like he hadn't even heard the curse words.

I put my hand on the door to get out, but I stopped when Bonbon started talking to the boy again.

"Don't reckond I need to tell you to come back?" he said.

The boy didn't answer. He was frowning and rubbing his forehead. I touched him with my knee.

"I'm coming back," he said.

Bonbon didn't see me do it, but he knew I had touched the boy; and now he just sat there looking at the boy like he expected to have trouble out of him. He raised his hand and pressed the silver button on the dash drawer and took out the gun.

"All right, Geam," he said.

My name is James Kelly, but Bonbon couldn't say James. He called me Geam. He was the only man, white or black, who called me Geam.

Bonbon got out the truck and I got out, too. We met at the front. The light was on us a second.

"Leave it here when I get back?" I asked him.

"Yeah. Put the keys in the dash drawer."

"Taking off," I said.

"See you tomorrow, Geam," he said.

He went in the yard and I got in the truck. I shot away from there just as fast as Bonbon had come down the quarter.

5

"That sonofabitch," the boy said.

"You'll get used to it," I said.

"Not me," he said. "If they think I'm go'n stay here any five years . . ."

"Oh, I see. One of them, huh?"

He didn't say any more. Now he was holding a handkerchief on his forehead. When I came out to the highway, I sat myself good behind the wheel. I wanted to get to Baton Rouge and back quickly as I could.

"Never seen you around here before," I said. "How did you get to know Marshall Hebert?"

"All right," he said. "If you want to know what happened you don't have to beat around the bush. Just come on out and ask me what happened."

"You don't have to get mad with me, buddy," I said. "All I have to do is drive you places."

"And ask questions," he said.

"You don't have to answer them," I said.

"Well, I killed somebody," he said. "Marshall Hebert bond me out. And you can tell him this—if you his whitemouth—if he think I'm serving any five years on that plantation he can just haul back and kiss my ass. I'm running 'way from there first chance I get."

"Like tonight?" I said.

"You'll never know, whitemouth," he said.

"Well, let me and you get one thing straight right now," I said. "I'm nobody's whitemouth. And another thing: if you want to run tonight I'll stop the truck right now and let you go. Did you hear me?"

He was quiet, still holding that handkerchief against his forehead.

"All right," I said. "We got that settled."

"Shit," he said, and laid back in the seat.

# 2

---

A half hour later I was crossing the Mississippi River into Baton Rouge. I could smell the strong odor from the cement plant down below the bridge. Sometimes the odor was so strong it nearly made you sick. Farther to the right were the chemical plants and oil companies. I could see hundreds and hundreds of electric lights over there. High above all the lights and buildings and oil tanks was a big blaze of fire. The fire came from a flamestack burning off wasted gas.

I woke up the boy and asked him where he lived. He told me to go to South Baton Rouge. I asked him where at in South Baton Rouge and he told me Louise Street. When I came to Louise Street I had to wake him up again. This time he sat up in the seat and nodded for me to go on. After I had gone about two blocks he pointed to a house on the right. I drove the truck to the side and parked before a little white cottage house. The front door was open and there was a light on inside.

"What all you have to get?" I asked the boy.

He didn't answer; he just got out and started toward the house. I got out of the truck and followed him. I wasn't doing it to keep an eye on him—that was his business if he wanted to run; I was going with him to help him bring the things back outside.

"Marcus," a woman said, soon as he walked into the room. "Mama, Marcus here."

"Didn't I tell you?" another person said. This was an old lady's voice. "Didn't I tell you?" she said again.

I came in the room and stood by the door. Everybody was so busy looking at Marcus, they didn't see me or hear me come in. An old lady who must have been eighty or ninety was patting Marcus on the face. Marcus didn't like it, but the old lady was so happy to see him she couldn't stop. Another, younger woman and a man were standing to the side. The young woman looked happy, but the man just looked disgusted. A little boy and a little girl stood on the other side of the man, looking at Marcus, too. Both of them acted like they were a little afraid of him. The little boy was the first to notice that somebody else had come in the room. After he had looked at me a second, everybody else did, too.

"You come for his clothes?" the old lady asked me.

"Yes ma'am; a bed too if you got one."

She nodded.

"I'm Miss Julie Rand," she said. "I christened Marcus."

"I'm James Kelly," I said, going up to her.

I shook hands with all of them. The man was called George and he was Miss Julie Rand's son. The young woman, Clorestine, was George's wife. Clorestine acted just the opposite from her husband. He was disgusted and ashamed of Marcus; she was happy to see Marcus was out of jail.

"I don't remember you," Miss Julie Rand said to me. "How long you live at Hebert?"

"The last three years."

"No, I had left by then," she said.

"Long before then, Mama," Clorestine said.

"Yes," the old lady said. She looked at Marcus again. "Hungry?" she asked him.

8

"Starving," he said. He didn't use any kind of kindness or respect in his voice. I could see George looking at him from the side. He hated Marcus for what he had done, and he was ashamed because I knew about it.

"Care to have supper with us, Mr. Kelly?" Miss Julie asked me. Miss Julie had a little, high-pitched voice just fitting for somebody about her size and age.

"No ma'am, I haven't so long ate."

"Well, there's some ice cream and pie there," she said. "You might have little dessert with us."

"I'm taking a bath," Marcus said. "Eat when I come out."

Everybody watched him leave the room. He started pulling the shirttail out of his pants before he reached the other door. The back of the shirt was smeared with dirt and there was a tear on the right sleeve. For about a minute after he left the room, nobody said a thing. Then the old lady looked up at me. I'm about six-feet-one and she was about four-eight or -nine, so she had to hold her head 'way back to look me in the face.

"He's a good boy," she said.

"Sure," I thought; "and handy with a knife, too." Because now I had figured out who he was. A colored boy had killed another colored boy at one of the honky-tonks over the weekend. What I couldn't figure out was where did Marshall Hebert fit into this.

"Come to my room with me, Mr. Kelly, will you, please?" Miss Julie said in that little, high-pitched voice that was so fitting for her.

I followed her into a small, ill-smelling room that had too much furniture. All old people who move from the country to the city live in rooms like these. They try to bring everything they had in the country and cram it into a little room

9

that can't hold half of what they own. Miss Julie had an old sofa chair against the wall and another little rocker by the bed. There was an old trunk by the window with a pile of quilts and blankets stacked on top of it. Against the other wall was an old armoire leaning to one side. There must have been a half dozen paste-board boxes stacked on top of the armoire. In the corner by the armoire were several paper bags packed full of clothes. The mantelpiece was cluttered with all kinds of nick-nacks, and there was an old coal oil lamp there, too, just in case the electric lights went out. No matter what wall you faced, you saw pictures of Jesus Christ. These pictures were on old calendars that Miss Julie Rand had never thrown away. They dated from the late thirties up to this year—forty-eight. Above the mantelpiece, stuck inside an old black wooden frame, was a picture of a man and a woman. The man was sitting; the woman was standing beside him. I figured that this was Miss Julie and her husband when she was much, much younger.

"Please, sit down, Mr. Kelly," she said.

So I sat in the sofa chair while she sat in her little rocker looking at me. She was a very small old lady, and now, sitting there with her feet hardly touching the floor, she looked even smaller. Her head was tied in an old pink rag, and her gray dress nearly touched the floor. The old brown slippers on her feet looked pretty near old as she did.

But the thing that hit me most about the room was the odor in there. It was the odor of old people, old clothes, old liniment bottles.

"From round here, Mr. Kelly?" she asked me.

"Pointe Coupee up there," I said.

"You look like a very nice person, Mr. Kelly," she said. Then she looked at me a long time, studying me closely. "Yes, a very nice person."

I didn't know if she wanted me to agree with her or not, but I know I didn't feel comfortable with her looking at me like that. And that odor in the room wasn't helping out matters, either.

"I want you do me a favor, Mr. Kelly," she said.

"Yes ma'am?"

"Look after Marcus up there."

"I'll do what I can."

"Sidney Bonbon still overseer there, I hear."

"Yes ma'am, he's still there."

"Still the same?"

"Most of us get along with him," I said.

"Yes," she said, nodding her head. "But first he got to try you, he got to break you. I want you talk to Marcus. I want you make him understand."

"I'll do what I can," I said.

I could still smell that odor. It came from everywhere in the room. I wanted to hold my breath, but the old lady was looking at me all the time.

"I hate to see him come there," she said. "But that pen can kill a man. There ain't much left to you when they let you go."

"That plantation can do the same to some people," I said.

"Yes, that's true," she said thoughtfully. "But you got the open air, and you got people who care round you."

"He'll make out all right if he take orders," I said. "But he'll have to take orders there."

"You can talk to him, Mr. Kelly. You look like a person he'll listen to."

"That one listen to anybody?" I thought. "You trying to kid me, little old lady?"

"Because he's a good boy," she said, looking at me like she didn't believe what she was saying herself. "That other boy was wrong. They forced him to fight that boy. That other boy was the first to pull his knife."

"How do you know all this?" I was thinking. "That happened about three in the morning and you probably had been in bed eight or nine hours already. You would believe anything he said, wouldn't you?"

"He don't have a mama or a daddy," she was saying. "His mama died and his daddy just ran off and left him. I did my best to raise him right, but you can see I'm old."

I nodded. That old lady could sure talk sorrowfully when she wanted to.

"You will look after him, won't you?" she said.

"I'll advise him," I said. "But I can't make him do what he don't want to do. I'll do my best."

"Yes, I appreciate that," she said. "I would go and stay with him myself, but my children don't want me on that plantation any more. I stay sick lately. Right now I'm very sick, Mr. Kelly."

"You look good," I said.

"Ahh, Mr. Kelly," she said, smiling. I could see she didn't have any teeth. Then she stopped smiling and just looked at me a while. "No, Mr. Kelly, it's only a matter of time now. But I've made peace with my Maker."

I didn't say anything, because I didn't know what to say. I didn't know what to do, either. I think I made a slight nod.

"How do you get along with Mr. Marshall?" she asked me.

"We speak when we meet," I said. "Other than that we don't have much to do with each other."

"Do you know Sidney Bonbon has something on him?"

"No ma'am, I didn't know that."

"Yes," she said, nodding. "That's why I had to leave. I had been the Hebert cook forty years. Cooked for three generations of them. Sidney Bonbon got something on him and put Pauline there in my place."

"What did Bonbon get on him?" I asked.

Miss Julie rocked in that little chair now nearly a minute, just studying me. She didn't want to tell me, I could see that, and maybe she had already said too much. You see, I was only thirty-three years old, still 'a child, and children shouldn't know too much about other people's business. Especially when it was about somebody important as Marshall Hebert. But Miss Julie needed me to look after Marcus, and she knew I knew how bad she needed me.

"Two people got killed long ago. People say Bonbon did it for Mr. Marshall . . ."

Miss Julie didn't stop rocking to say this. You could see how much she hated to say it or even think about it. She didn't tell me to keep it to myself, but her eyes warned me to never repeat it again. She went on rocking in that little chair, her old brown slippers barely touching the floor.

"So that's it," I thought. "So that's why Bonbon steals half of everything that grows on that plantation. Marshall can't do a thing about it. So that's—but wait. Wait just one minute. You know about it, too, don't you? Is that the reason he got Marcus out of jail?" I had been trying to figure out something all the way from Hebert into Baton Rouge. "Why?" I kept on asking myself. "Why? Who is this boy and why?" I knew that white men bonded colored boys out of jail for a few hundred dollars and worked them until they had gotten all their money back two and three times over. But I was trying to figure out why Marshall Hebert would do this when he already had more people than he needed. Now I knew. This little old lady had the finger on him, too.

"No, it's not what you thinking, Mr. Kelly," she said.

"That white man been good to me. I went to him 'cause I didn't have nowhere else to turn."

I nodded, but I didn't believe her. To me she was a little old gangster just like Bonbon was. She was even worst than Bonbon. Bonbon was white and you expect this of white people. But she was my own race—and a woman, too.

"Sidney still messing round with Pauline down the quarter?" Miss Julie asked.

"Yes ma'am," I said, eying her just like I would any other gangster.

"How are those children?"

"Pretty big boys."

"And his own wife up the quarter, she got any?"

"That one little girl," I said.

She nodded. "He's more crazy 'bout Pauline than he is his own wife," she said.

"Pauline knows that," I said.

"Huh," Miss Julie said. Then she started looking at me like she knew more about life than somebody like me would ever know. "You think there will ever be a time?" she asked.

I didn't know what she was talking about.

"When him and Pauline will be able to live together like they want."

"They live pretty good already," I said.

"Still go and come like he want?"

"Just like he want."

"And his wife know all about it?"

"Yes ma'am. All she got to do is come to that gate and look down the quarter. She can see that truck or that horse down there almost any time he's not home."

"I feel sorry for her, not for Pauline," Miss Julie said. "Pauline go'n look after herself. That other one, I don't think she got 'nough sense to do it."

14

We got quiet after that. Miss Julie was rocking in that little chair and studying me again. Her little old black, wrinkled face was sad and thoughtful, but at the same time very wise. I'm sure she knew everything about me already. She knew I would look after Marcus, she knew I wouldn't say anything about Marshall and Bonbon—though I was sure everybody on the plantation knew about it just like she did. Miss Julie looked at me so long, I turned my head and looked at the pictures on the wall. I wasn't interested in her biblical pictures, I just didn't feel comfortable with her looking at me like that. Old people look at you like that for two reasons. One, when you've done something wrong. The other is when they want you to do something for them. The thing they want you to do usually turns out to be a burden. The heavier the burden, the longer they look at you. And Miss Julie looked at me a long, long time.

"Yes," she said, like she was sure of me now. I didn't look at her, because I knew why she had said it. She said it once more, then she stopped the chair from rocking "Marcus ought to be through bathing. Let's go eat some ice cream."

I was so glad she had said that I nearly jumped out of that chair. But I had enough good manners to let her go out of the room before I did.

# 3

Marcus was through bathing, all right; he had even put on a suit and he was sitting at the table, eating. Clorestine brought me and Miss Julie some ice cream and pie to the table. George and the children were sitting on the couch, looking through a magazine.

"You planning on going somewhere?" I asked Marcus.

"A short piece," he said.

"Yes?" I said.

"Yes," he said, looking at me.

He had on a white sharkskin suit. His shirt and his tie were blue, but the tie little darker than the shirt. A silver tie clip held the tie and the shirt together. Marcus looked at me for about long as it take you to chew two or three times, then he turned from me again. He thought he had got his point over. I looked at the old lady who had been saying what a good boy he was.

"You won't be long, will you, Marcus?" she said. "That boy might have friends out there and they might . . ."

She stopped because he wasn't even listening. When he got through eating, he got up from the table and went to George sitting on the couch.

"Borrow your keys, George?" he said.

George didn't answer him; he didn't even look at him.

"George, can I borrow the keys to your car?" Marcus said again.

George raised his head this time.

"You think you doing the right thing?" he said. "That white man done put up money to get you out and—"

"Man, just lend me the keys," Marcus said. "You don't have to preach to me."

George got the keys out of his pocket and handed them to Marcus. I thought I had seen and heard enough, and when he went out the door I went after him. I caught up with him just as he went down the steps.

"A second," I said.

"Hurry up," he said. "I'm late."

"Where you think you're going, Marcus?"

"I got a date," he said.

"You got a date on that plantation," I said.

"I'll see you later," he said, turning to leave.

I jerked him back around.

"Don't you never do that no more," he said, threatening me.

"What would you do, boy? What?"

"Plenty," he said.

I got so mad with him then, I wanted to slam him up against that truck. I had raised my hands to grab him when I noticed Miss Julie had come to the door. Marcus turned from me and went to the car and drove up the street. I stood there watching the car until it had turned left on the other street; then I went back inside.

"Be little patient with him, he's all right," Miss Julie said.

"He'll pay for it, not me," I said.

"What y'all doing in the field, now?" George asked me.

"Pulling corn," I said. I sat at the table and started eating again.

"That's some mean work, huh?" George asked.

"I drive the tractor and I have an umbrella," I said. "The ones walking behind that trailer got the mean part of it."

"You can't tell him nothing," George said.

"You got to have little patient," Miss Julie said.

"Patient, patient, patient," George said. "You been saying patient ever since he been staying here. It ain't done a bit o' good."

"And suppose you didn't have a mama to raise you, you think you be any better?"

"I'd least listen to people trying to help me," George said.

"Marcus is a good boy," Miss Julie said, eating ice cream. "He's a good boy," she said again.

Marcus got back around midnight, and by the time we finished loading the truck it was twelve thirty. George and Clorestine and the children had gone to bed long ago, but Miss Julie had waited up with me. She went to Marcus and put her arms around him and started crying when he got ready to leave. She told him to be sure to come back and see her next week sometime. She told him if he didn't come to see her, then she was coming to see him. Marcus didn't say a word. He let her hold him and cry over him, but he didn't open his mouth. She followed us to the door and waved again just before I drove away. Marcus didn't even look back; he just sat there like he was half dead. From the way his clothes was smelling, I wouldn't have doubted he wasn't.

When we got back to the plantation, I helped Marcus unload his clothes and the bed. There wasn't any light in the room so I loaned him an old lantern that I had in the kitchen. We put the bed together, then I took the truck back up the quarter. Bonbon's house and the yard were black and quiet. The dog didn't even bark when I parked the truck there. I put the keys in the dash drawer and went back down the quarter. Marcus was still up when I came to the house. I went to my room and got ready for bed.

"There ain't a closet or a chifforobe or nothing in here," he said, from the other side.

"You can hang those things up tomorrow," I said.

"I want put them up tonight," he said.

I didn't say any more because I was mad already for staying in Baton Rouge so long. I got on my knees and made the Sign of the Cross, then I got into bed. Long time ago I used to say the whole prayer, but that was long ago when I was young and when I thought the Old Man was going to do it all for me. But now I know I have to do it for myself. Still, I make the Sign of the Cross every night to stay in practice. Who knows? Maybe I'll go back to the full thing again some day.

"You got a hammer and some nails?" Marcus said. He was in my room now, standing right over my head. I could smell that whore reek in his clothes.

"Get out of here, boy," I told him. "If you don't want to sleep, please, let me sleep."

"I got to hang up my clothes," he said.

"Hang them up where?" I said.

"I found this," he said, holding it over my face. I couldn't see what it was, but I figured it was a piece of wire.

"You figuring on doing any nailing here tonight? You know it's after one o'clock?"

"I got to hang up my clothes," he said.

I looked up at him in the dark. I could hardly see him, but I could smell that whore reek in his clothes.

"Go back there in the kitchen and turn that light on," I

said. "You'll find a hammer and a can of nails under the table. Go round there and do all the nailing you want. But I'm jerking your ass out of that bed tomorrow morning at four thirty."

Marcus got the things out of the kitchen and went back to his side and started nailing. He must have nailed against that wall a whole hour before he had strung up that one little piece of wire.

# 4

Billie Jean used to shake me a long time to get me up in the morning, but now my Billie is gone and I have to make it by myself. Where are you, Billie Jean, and what are you doing now, my little chicken? Wherever you are, whatever you're doing, I hope you're making him happy as you used to make me. It was good then, wasn't it? It was up near Pointe Coupee, and it was good, wasn't it? But my little chicken wanted New Orleans—Pointe Coupee was too slow; and once she got in New Orleans she wanted more than what daddy could give her. So baby found another prince. Well, that's the way it rolls; that's the way it rolls. Daddy's got nothing against you, baby. Daddy understands about life, he always have. Little chickens need fur coats, perfume, silk dresses and silk drawers; and when daddy can't afford these things, chicken must look somewhere else. Well, that's the way it goes, and God go with you, little chicken.

I sat on the side of the bed, thinking about her and remembering four, five, six years back. Remembering the nights coming in from the field and the big tub of hot water waiting for me, and Billie washing my back, and then us in that old Ford, heading for town. And dancing and dancing until late, and then hurrying back to that bed and loving, loving, loving until morning. Then hitting that field again, half dead, and then back, and the tub of hot water, and the dancing, and the loving. For how many years—two? three?—then it was over. Daddy wasn't able to keep up the pace, and baby had to find somebody who could. Is daddy bitter? No, daddy's not bitter at all. All that's part of this big old thing called life. Daddy is not bitter, baby. Come back now and he'll say yes to you. Maybe that's why he hangs around here. It reminds him a little of the old place, and he figures that one day you might pass by and decide to stop, and then . . . Stop dreaming, Frank James Kelly. It's getting close to five o'clock and another day is breaking.

I made the Sign of the Cross, not the whole prayer, and got into my khakis. After cooking up some grits and eggs and making a big pot of coffee, I sat in the back door and ate breakfast. The sun hadn't come up yet, but there was still enough light out there to see. I could see how the dew made the grass bend over. I could see my little gray pecan tree, my old leaning picket fence, and the old toilet that looked like it was ready to tumble over with the first light breeze. "One of these Saturdays I'm going to fix it," I told myself. But I had been saying that a couple of years now and I still hadn't done a thing.

I could hear the rest of the quarter getting up, too. I could hear Aunt Emma feeding her chickens and hollering at Saint Mark Brown's dog, saying, "You trifling thing, get away from here; get away from here, you trifling thing. You worser than that old paw-owner yours."

A second later I heard the dog hollering; then I heard Saint Mark Brown saying, "Leave that dog 'lone, you god-damn hag." And I could hear Aunt Emma saying: "Then keep him out this yard. Keep him 'way from my chickens, the old egg eater." And farther up the quarter and farther down the quarter I could hear the rest of the place getting up, too.

The sun wasn't up yet, but it was getting lighter and lighter, and I knew it was about time I got up the quarter and cranked up Red Hannah. But first I had to get Playboy on his feet. So I got myself a cold drink of water, then I poured up another cupful to take round the other side. I had to go back through my front room and across the gallery to come into his room. And, oh, he had everything hanging so pretty-like. He had his suits, his shirts, his ties all on a little line. Then he had six or seven pairs of dress shoes up against the wall in a nice little row. Then he had his suitcases stacked neatly in the corner. And him? Sleeping. Laying there snoring like a six-month-old baby. I looked down at him a few seconds, then I kicked against the bed.

"All right, hit it."

He didn't move; didn't budge; didn't even grunt.

I shook him. "All right, let's go."

He grunted this time, but he didn't move. I shook him again. He grunted, but he didn't move. So I grabbed him by the shoulder and rolled him off that bed down on the floor. He laid there looking up at me and rubbing his eyes. Since I had brought the cup of cold water in there, I thought I might as well use it; so I calmly poured it over his still-sleepy face. That woke him up, all right; he jumped up with his fist ready. I had put the cup on the mantelpiece and I was ready for him.

"Well?" I said.

"I'm go'n get you for that," he said.

"What's stopping you now?" I said.

"I'm go'n get you," he said. "You just wait and see."

"Sure," I said. "You can use my washpan in the kitchen

to finish washing your face. I've got some food on the stove if you want to eat. You better if you know what's good for you."

"I don't need nobody to feed me."

"Uh-huh," I said. "I have some khakis round there, too; pants and shirt. They might be a little big, but there won't be any womenfolks watching you out there."

"If you trying to buy your way out, you better think about something else," he said.

"Uh-huh," I said. "Listen, I'm going up there to get that tractor. By the time I get back I expect you to be through eating—that's if you want to eat—and I expect you to be waiting out there at that gate."

"Or you go'n put your white boss on me, whitemouth?"

"I'm trying to keep him off your ass," I said. "You can take my advice or you can forget it, that's up to you."

I went to the door and looked back at him again. He was still watching me.

"Clothes and food round the other side—and you be waiting at that gate," I said. "If I leave you in the quarter and he bring you back there in that truck, you'll cuss the day your mon brought you in this world. And you might do that before all this is over with."

He was still watching me when I left the room.

# 5

By the time I had lubed Red Hannah and given her enough fuel and water, that sun was slipping up behind the trees. When I came back down the quarter, I saw John and Freddie waiting for me in front of John's house. John and Freddie were two punks. John was the big punk, Freddie was the little one. Together they pulled more corn than any other two men I had ever seen; in church on Sunday they shouted more than any two women. The funny thing about it, John and Freddie were ushers in church and they were supposed to look after the women when the women started shouting. But it always ended up with everybody else looking after John and Freddie. A couple of good-size women could hold down Freddie when he started shouting, but it always took seven or eight men to hold down big John.

John and Freddie hopped in the trailer before the tractor had stopped good. Then, as I came farther down the quarter, I saw Playboy Marcus coming out the yard. He had on a short-sleeve green shirt and a pair of brown pants. No hat—not even a handkerchief round his neck. He had on a pair of brown and white dress shoes.

"Where the hell you think you're going in that?" I asked him.

He didn't answer me; he didn't even glance my way. He got in the front trailer because John and Freddie were in the other one. John and Freddie, in their big straw hats and khakis, were looking at him. They wanted to laugh (they were the laughing-est two you ever saw), but you could see they were afraid of him.

"You better get back in there, boy, and put something else on," I told Marcus.

He didn't move.

"There's a hat in my room on that armoire, Marcus," I said.

He still didn't move. I jumped off the tractor and ran inside to get the straw hat because I was already late. While I was in there I got a khaki shirt too and brought it out and threw it in the trailer where he was. He didn't pick up either one; he didn't even glance down at them; he just stood there with his arms folded and his back against the side of the trailer.

I put Red Hannah in gear and started out for the field. The whole quarter was up now. The people who didn't have to go in the field for Marshall Hebert were getting ready to go out in their own little patches. Besides corn-pulling time, this was the cotton-picking season, too. And most of the women you saw now wore old dresses and big yellow straw hats with a piece of rag or handkerchief under the hat.

The plantation (or what was left of the plantation now) had all its crop far back in the field. The front land was for the sharecroppers. The Cajuns had the front-est and best land, and the colored people (those who were still hanging on) had the middle and worst land. The plantation land was farther back still, almost to the swamps. We had to pass through three different gates, through a cow pasture (in the early morning the cows were lazy and didn't want to move out your way), before we got to the patch of corn where we were working today.

I parked the end-trailer up the headland, then I swung Red Hannah down a set of rows. John and Freddie took the two side rows and gave Marcus the flat row in the middle. That was the easiest row because the corn was already down and all you had to do was walk there and jerk it off the stalk. But even giving Marcus the easiest row, they knew they could kill him off any time they wanted to. They started slow, just talking and giggling between the two of them. "Child, you know this; child, you know that—" and then all of a sudden they would bust out laughing at something that only they knew about. But Marcus, back of the trailer in his short-sleeve green shirt and brown pants, wasn't saying a thing. The hat and the long-sleeve khaki shirt I had brought out the house were still in the trailer where I had thrown them.

"Just wait," I thought. "Just wait. Before this day is over—hah . . ."

Marcus stuck pretty close with John and Freddie on the first trailer, but soon as we had loaded it and started on the second one, I could see them picking up speed. They weren't going fast—no, that was coming later this evening when Bonbon was out there. Right now they were going about three-fourths, the way a good pitcher go in the sixth or seventh inning when he's leading by a comfortable amount of runs. But even that three-fourths speed was starting to tell on Marcus. Already he was starting to jerk on one ear of corn two or three times before he broke it from the stalk. Couple times there he dropped so far back, he couldn't even reach the trailer throwing the corn overhand.

The best way to pull corn is snatch it with one jerk and flip it underhand into the trailer or the wagon. But when you get so far back where you can't go underhand, then you got to go overhand, and that's when it start telling on you.

Because to draw that corn back over your shoulder and throw it like that, you use twice the energy. And I don't care how good you are, how strong you are, by the time you go a day like that it's going to be telling on you. So it was like that with Marcus. Each time he threw it from over his shoulder, it took just a little bit more from what he was going to need the rest of the day. And that whiskey he had drunk last night and that pussy he had wallowed in last night, and that no-sleeping and that no-eating and that short-sleeve green shirt and them thin, brown pants and that white, hot bitch way up in the sky were all working together against him to make matters worse. Every now and then I stopped when he got too far back. While I'd be waiting for him to catch up, John and Freddie would get together on the shady side of the trailer and talk and giggle and slap each other on the back like they hadn't seen each other in about ten years. Then soon as he had caught up, they would move back on their rows, never giving him one second of rest. By the time we had finished that second load, Marcus was so tired I thought he was going to drop before he got up on the trailer. But he made it, and we hooked up the other trailer and started toward the front for dinner.

# 6

When we came up to the house, I told Marcus to go in and eat and rest himself. He hopped off the tractor and staggered toward the gate. I went up the quarter and let John and Freddie off; then I took the two loads of corn up to the yard. The other two trailers were empty as usual. After I had parked the loaded ones in front of the crib and had fueled and watered Red Hannah for this evening, I hooked up the two empty ones and started on back down the quarter. Marcus was sitting on the gallery when I came to the house.

"You ate?" I asked him.

"I ain't got nothing in there."

"I got enough," I said.

"I don't want nothing for free."

"It's not free," I said. "You can pay me back later."

I went in and washed my face and hands and warmed up some beans and rice I had in the icebox. Then I dished up two platefuls and set one plate on the table, and I sat in the back door, eating. After a while, Marcus came back there. I nodded toward the plate. He washed his hands and sat down at the table.

"Gave you a pretty rough time, huh?" I said.

"Shit," he said. "I got news for all of them. That overseer and Marshall Hebert, too."

"Yes?" I said.

"They think I'm go'n stay on this fucking place any five years, they got another thought coming."

"They figure it'll be about seven years," I said. "After you get through charging at the store, it might be more than that."

"Shit," he said. "Seven years from now I won't even remember the name Hebert."

"When you figuring on running?" I said.

"You won't know the day or the hour," he said.

"I might tell, huh?"

"Just 'cause I'm eating your food don't say I trust you," he said.

I ate and looked out in the yard. It was a good ninety degrees out there. The grass that was bent over with dew this morning was standing straight up now.

"Soon as they have that little fifteen cents trial, I'm picking my chance," Marcus said.

"Why don't you run now?" I said.

"Uh-uh, they looking for that. I'll wait till they forget all about it."

I looked up at him.

"You got it all figured out?"

"I had it all figured out when I walked out of jail," he said. "Shit, you don't think I come here to stay, do you?"

"Yes, I think you come here to stay," I said. "I know you come here to stay."

"Shit," he said. "They don't nut this kid like they done nut all the rest of y'all round here."

"I still have mine," I said.

He didn't say anything, but I could see he didn't believe me.

"That boy you killed don't mean a thing, does it?"

"Nigger come on you with a knife, what you suppose to do, just stand there? Get him 'fore he get you."

"You got a lot to learn in this world," I told him.

"I done forgot more than plenty people'll ever know," he said.

"Sure," I said.

"Don't worry," he said. "I'll pay you back your food."

"Anytime," I said. "I'm not going anywhere."

He ate.

"How much they go'n pay me for working?" he asked.

"They don't pay 'bond people' anything," I said. "They feed you, they clothe you. If you want anything else, you can charge it at the store out there. That adds to your time."

"And they think I'm go'n stay here? Shit," he said.

"If I was you, I'd pick up some clothes at the store this evening," I said.

"You mean that shit I see y'all wearing round here?" he asked.

"Yes, that's the shit I'm talking about," I said.

"I'll never put that convict shit on my back," he said. "I'm used to silk."

When I got through eating I got up and put my plate in the dishpan on the stove.

"Well, I'm going to take myself a good nap," I said. "Round two we'll hit it again."

He sat there eating and looking out in the yard. I wanted to feel sorry for Marcus, but God knows he didn't help you.

"You better get yourself some rest, too," I said. "John

31

and Freddie were playing this morning. They won't be playing this evening when Bonbon come out there."

"Them two freaks and Bonbon can all kiss my ass," he said.

"Just thought I'd mention it, buddy," I said. "See you in a couple hours."

It was too hot to lay down on the bed, so I went out on the gallery. Ten minutes after I laid down I was sound to sleep. Round two, maybe a couple minutes before two, I was up again.

# 7

It was hot, it was burning up. You could see little monkeys dancing out there in front of you.

I got myself a cold drink of water and filled up that gallon jug and took it out to the tractor. By the time I had cranked up Red Hannah, I saw John and Freddie coming down the quarter. They were walking close together and just giggling. I didn't see how any two people, punks or no punks, could find anything to giggle about in all this heat; but there they were in their khakis and big straw hats and brogans, just giggling. You would have thought they were two little per-fumed gals going to the dance.

Marcus slid off the gallery and came out of the yard. I had climbed up on the tractor and John and Freddie had got in that end-trailer, and we watched Marcus coming to-ward us. He wore the same short-sleeve green shirt and brown pants; the same low-top shoes, and not a thing on his head.

"Where's that hat?" he asked me.

"You going to need more than a hat, boy," I said.

"Where's the hat?" he asked again.

"Under that load of corn at the front," I said.

"You got another one?"

"I got an old felt hat hanging on the chair in there, you want that?"

"No," he said.

"I got this red handkerchief in my pocket."

"I don't want no fucking red handkerchief," he said.

"Hop in," I said. "We're wasting time."

He got into the front trailer and we started for the field. I drove slowly through the quarter—I didn't want dust flying all over the place; but after I crossed the railroad tracks, I threw Red Hannah into high gear and let her take us to the back.

Lord, it was hot out there; Lord, it was hot. But I had something going for me. I had the big umbrella and I had something to dream about and forget the heat. I knew Red Hannah would stay in the road for me even if I slept a whole minute, so every now and then, to forget the sun and the dust, I thought back to the good times with Billie Jean. I thought about the tub, and I thought about us dancing, then I thought about us hurrying back to that bed. Sometimes we didn't make it back to the house; sometimes it happened right there in the car, sometimes in the open field. Once when it was over, we just kept on laying out there. Must have been a billion stars in the sky, and that big moon, like a tub of clean water, hung over our heads like it was there just for me and her. We laid there and laid there, and the next thing we knew it was morning and the people were coming in the field. Everybody bust out laughing when they saw us, and all we could do was laugh with them.

Then it was New Orleans, then it was over.

Freddie opened the first gate; John opened the second gate; Freddie opened the third one. Marcus didn't get down once until we reached the patch of corn.

"Here," I said, giving him my straw hat. "You better put that on."

He took the hat; no thanks, no nothing; he just took it. I got out my red handkerchief and tied it round my head. After all, I had the big umbrella, too.

So we started on down, Marcus in the middle and John and Freddie on the sides. They still weren't working too fast—fast enough to keep a step or two ahead of him—but still not fast as they could if they wanted to. But that was part of the plan. They were going to work him down gradually on the first load, and the last load, when Bonbon was there, they were going to really pour it on. I moved the tractor down the field slowly as I could—for his sake—but at the same time I had to go fast enough to get the work done. Three men were supposed to pull two loads of corn in the morning and two loads in the evening, and if they didn't get it done, Bonbon knew it was the driver who was stalling. So I had to keep up a pretty good speed, and at the same time not too fast so he would never fall too far back.

Somewhere between four and quarter after, we had the first trailer done. When I took it to the headland to unhook it and hook up the empty one, I looked across the patch of corn and saw Bonbon on the stallion.

# 8

By the time I had set the tractor down the field, Bonbon was there. His khaki shirt was wringing wet with sweat. His white straw hat was turned up at the sides like a cowboy hat; he even wore cowboy boots. His Winchester hung on the left side of the saddle; a crocker sack was tied on the right side of the saddle. A piece of grass rope was tied on the end of the sack, and I knew what to expect later.

Nobody said anything. Usually he spoke when he came out in the field like this, but this time he didn't. I set the tractor down the row; John and Freddie got on both sides of the trailer, Marcus got right behind it on the center row, and Bonbon got right behind Marcus on the stallion. The horse was so close to Marcus, I'm sure Marcus could feel the horse's hot breath on the back of his neck. So now it had started. Now they were going to give him a taste of what it meant to kill and then let yourself be bonded out of jail. They were going to let him know (not that they cared a hoot for the other boy) that he wasn't tough as he thought he was.

So now it had started. I set the tractor at the speed she's supposed to run when she has three men pulling corn behind her. John and Freddie started pitching corn like they had come into this world to do just that. And poor Marcus, with that black stallion only a step behind him, tried to keep up with them. He did for a while. He did for a row, a row and a half, then two. But soon as we started down the third set, I could see that that whiskey and that pussy from last night had caught up with him. And seeing that he was falling back, the two punks really poured it on.

"Move up," Freddie called.

Before I had gone fifty feet down the row, Marcus had dropped back fifteen; and before I had gone fifty more, he had dropped back that much farther. Now he was throwing that corn overhand, and with that trailer just a little over half full, I knew that was the end of him.

"Move up," Freddie called.

And I set Red Hannah at a little faster speed. Well, I had done all I could do for him. I had tried to bring him back here last night, I had fed him, I had given him a straw hat and even offered him khakis to wear. I had done everything a good Christian (one who had once believed) could do.

I glanced back now, and there were John and Freddie only about five feet behind the trailer. And back about thirty or thirty-five feet was Marcus. That short-sleeve shirt was wringing wet; that straw hat looked like it was wringing wet, too, though I'm not too sure I've ever seen a wringing wet straw hat from sweat alone. And there was Bonbon leaning on the pommel of the saddle, looking down at Marcus. And there was that black stallion about six inches behind Marcus—and poor Marcus feeling the horse's hot breath on the back of his neck.

"Move up," Freddie called.

I looked toward the front again. Old Hannah kept up her *putt-putt-putting* on down the row like nothing was happening. And those hot, burning, yellow stalks of corn stood before us and all around us like nothing was happening.

And that old sun to my right—white, small, and still strong—shone down on us like nothing was happening. Man, man, man, I thought; only you worry about what's happening to you, because nothing or anybody else cares. And you, Billie, you care? Do you care at all, my little chicken? And how about the one he laid with last night, and how about the ones he bought drinks for on Saturday before he killed that boy? Do they care? And how about You, do You care? I don't think so—because if You did, it looks to me like You would send us a little breeze, wouldn't You? Now, mind you, I'm not asking You that for myself. Not at all, not at all. I figure a man with an eight-grade education, with a sitting-down job, shouldn't go round complaining about anything. But it's for the others I want it. Especially for the one 'way back there.

I stopped when I got to the end and looked back, and he already had the sack hanging on his shoulder. It had happened like this. I wasn't there, now, I was here on the tractor; but I had seen it happen before and I knew what had taken place.

"All right," Bonbon had said. "Your arm getting tired. Here, try this."

He had untied the sack and thrown it down on the ground before Marcus. Marcus had picked it up and looked at it, but he didn't know what he was supposed to do.

"Look it over good," Bonbon had probably said. "It be part of you 'fore that sun go down there."

Marcus had probably stood there fumbling with it a minute, while all the time Bonbon had leaned a little on the pommel of the saddle, looking down at him. The horse had stood there sweating a little and hoping that Marcus would hurry up and find out what the sack was about so he could start moving again. He didn't mind carrying Bonbon (he was born to carry man), but he would rather move with Bonbon or two like Bonbon than stand with one Bonbon in that hot sun.

Marcus finally understood what the sack was about and slipped it over his shoulder. Now he started pulling corn and putting it in the sack. He was so weak now he had to jerk on an ear of corn sometimes three times before he could break it off. A dozen ears of corn in the sack, and already the sack felt like it weighed a hundred pounds. Already the rope had started to eat through that green shirt at his shoulder. Five more ears of corn, and the sack felt twice as heavy. Five more, and poor Marcus could hardly move. And Bonbon never saying a word, just leaning a little on the pommel of the saddle like he had all the time in the world.

Marcus staggered when he tried to swing the sack on his back, so he dropped it on the ground and dragged it toward the tractor. I had parked the tractor on the headland, John and Freddie had moved up against the trailer in the shade, and the three of us watched Marcus dragging the sack toward the end. When he came up to the tractor he rested about ten seconds, then he swung the sack up on the trailer. He climbed up and dumped it, then he jumped back down and went back down the row. Bonbon hadn't moved—I ought to say the horse hadn't moved—Bonbon had straightened up in the saddle and he was watching a hawk flying in the sky just to his right. There was a little pecan tree fifty or sixty yards farther down the headland, and the hawk flew there and rested on one of the top limbs. Bonbon let him rest a minute, like he wanted to give him a fair shake; then I saw him pulling the Winchester slowly out of the sling and raising it to his shoulder. The first shot chipped off piece of the limb, just close enough to make the hawk fly away. The hawk broke from the tree and flew across the field. I saw Bonbon moving the rifle slowly and I saw the sun on the barrel (blue-like) and my eyes went to the hawk. I heard the *pi-yow-yow* of the Winchester, and I saw two or three feathers busting away from the hawk, and I saw the hawk coming down over the field like a wet shirt that somebody had thrown up in the air.

"Chicken there, Freddie," Bonbon called to the headland.

"Yassuh," Freddie said, already running over to where the hawk had come down.

Bonbon put the rifle back and touched the horse lightly to make him move. By the time Freddie got back with the hawk, Marcus and Bonbon had got to the end and Marcus had climbed up on the trailer to dump his sack.

"Where I get him?" Bonbon asked Freddie.

"Poor little thing ain't got no more heart," Freddie said.

All of us looked at Freddie holding the hawk up in the air. The hawk was mostly gray and brown, but there were some red and black feathers across its wings and its back. When I said all of us were looking at the hawk, I should have said all of us were looking at the hawk except Marcus. Marcus was looking at Bonbon. He had probably glanced at the hawk once, but he started looking at Bonbon after. But I didn't know it then. It wasn't until later I knew he had been looking at Bonbon a long time.

"Had the pistol I could get him with that," Bonbon said.

"Pistol go that far, Mr. Sidney?" Freddie asked. He was still holding the hawk up so everybody could see it.

"Pistol can go, you just got to know how to shoot it," Bonbon said.

"If anybody can, you can, Mr. Sidney," Freddie said.

"I do all right," Bonbon said.

Then I saw him turning and looking at Marcus. He didn't look straight at him, he looked at him from the side. And from the way Marcus stood there looking back at Bonbon, I could tell he had been looking at him a long time. So it was Bonbon who let me know Marcus had been looking at him and not at the hawk. And it was the look in Marcus's face that let me know Bonbon hadn't given the hawk a break when he didn't shoot him on the limb; he had shot twice because he wanted to show Marcus how good he was.

Bonbon turned from Marcus and looked across the field at the sun. I could hear the *sagg-sagg* of the saddle when he shifted his weight from one side to the other.

"Move her, Geam," he said.

Freddie tied his hawk on the back of the trailer with a piece of twine, and Marcus tied his sack on the back of the trailer by the rope. We started back down the field, and Marcus kept up with them about halfway down. Then he fell back and had to get the sack again. Bonbon and the horse were right behind him all the way.

# 9

When we got to the front it was dark already. Everybody else had come out the field, and you could see the smoke flying out the kitchen chimleys where the women were cooking supper, and you could see the men sitting or laying down on the gallery, waiting for the food to get done so they could eat. I dropped Marcus off at the house; then I went up to Freddie's house and let him and his girlfriend off; then I went on up to the yard. My other two trailers had been emptied and pulled to the side, so now I parked the two full trailers before the crib. That's how it went. You brought two trailerfuls at noon and the boys emptied them that evening. Then you brought two trailerfuls that night and the boys emptied them the next morning. It went on like that until you got through; then you went into hay. But hay was out of the question for at least another month.

After I had unhooked Red Hannah from the two trailers, I parked her over by the toolshop and went over to the store to get something for supper. The store was packed full of people. Old Godeau (with his clubfoot) and his son Ferdinand moved from one counter to the other. I knew I couldn't get waited on right then, so I went around the other side and had myself a couple beers. You could buy soft drinks in the store or if you were a white man you could drink a beer in there, but if you were colored you had to go to the little side room—"the nigger room." I kept telling myself, "One of these days I'm going to stop this, I'm going to stop this; I'm a man like any other man and one of these days I'm going to stop this." But I never did. Either I was too thirsty to do it, or after I had been working in the field all day I was just too tired and just didn't care. So I went around there and had a beer with Burl, Snuke, and a couple others from the quarter. They asked me about Marcus and how he made out with Bonbon today. I told them all right. They looked at me, waiting to hear more, but I didn't have any more to say. Then Tick-Tock came in and I bought her a beer. Tick-Tock was a single gal in the quarter and she would give you a piece if you treated her right. I had gotten couple pieces from her myself. But we didn't have anything going for us; it was just friendly. I needed a piece at the time and I asked her for it and she said yes. I didn't give her any money because she didn't want any money. But any time I caught her out somewhere I would buy her a drink, or if I saw her at one of the house fairs I would buy her a bowl of gumbo or a fish dinner. Now I bought her a beer, and we leaned on the counter drinking and talking. She hadn't been home since leaving the cotton field, and I could see sweat marks down the side of her face. Somebody put a nickel in the jukebox and asked her to dance. She danced with him and came back where I was. I bought her another beer and left.

When I came home I saw Marcus laying on the gallery. He looked like somebody had beat him with an eight-plait whip and left him there to die.

"Hey,' I called to him. "Hey, there."

He raised up slowly and looked at me.

43

"Brought you a beer," I said. "Come on in."

He got up real slowly and followed me inside. I turned on the light and opened the bottle of beer for him. He took it and sat down at the table. I could see how that rope had ate through the shoulder of that green shirt.

"Why don't you take a bath," I said. "You'll feel better."

"You a freak or something?" he said.

I went up to him and snatched the beer out of his hand and threw it out the window.

"Now, get the fuck out of here," I said. "Get out."

"I'm sorry," he said.

"You're not sorry, you rotten sonofabitch. You think somebody got to kiss your ass to get along with you."

"What you expect?" he said. "Don't get mad? Look at me. Look at the blisters in my hands. I been working like a mule all day."

"You should have thought about that before you killed that boy."

"He was go'n kill me," Marcus said, his voice getting a little higher than it ought to be. "Ain't I done said a thousand times he was go'n kill me? What I was suppose to do, stand there and let him kill me first?"

"Then you should have kept your ass in Bayonne," I said. "I'm getting tired of this shit."

"I said I was sorry. What you want a man to say?"

I stood there looking at him. I was sorry I had hollered at him now.

"I'll get out," he said. But he was getting up slowly, hoping I would tell him to stay.

"Sit down," I said. "You got another beer there. You can either drink it now or with your food."

"Can I have it now?"

I opened it and gave it to him; then I started cooking. I

44

had bought a pound of sausage, and I already had tomatoes and onions at the house; so I threw all that together and put on a pot of rice to go with it. I usually ate before I bathed, but since he was there to watch the pot, I went on and took my bath. The food was ready by the time I got out the tub and put on my clothes.

"I ain't cut out for this kind of life, Jim," Marcus said.

"No?" I said.

"Look at me," he said, looking down at his clothes. "This ain't me."

"It's you," I said.

"I can't go on like this," he said, looking up at me again.

"You can," I said. "Others do."

"Not me," he said.

"Well, you should have thought about that before you pulled that knife," I said.

"How many times I done told you he pulled his knife first?" Marcus said, his voice getting high again. He had a nice voice until he got excited, then it got high. "How many times I done told you that, Jim?" he said.

"Yeah, you told me," I said. "How's the food?"

"It's good."

"It keeps me going," I said.

"You all right, Jim," Marcus said. "I'm sorry what I say. Don't pay me no mind."

"Forget it," I said.

"Look at me," he said, holding out his hands. "I can't even hold a fork right."

I looked at his hands. Both of them were blistered and raw.

"Soak them in some warm salt water," I said.

"That help?"

"Help some."

"How 'bout my shoulders?"

"Bathe it in some salt water. I'll give you a towel. And tomorrow wear another piece of rag over your shoulder. Keep you from bruising it."

"Jesus, have mercy," Marcus said. "Did he have to put that rope on the sack? Couldn't he put a strap or something?"

"It won't kill you," I said.

"No, I ain't go'n die, that's for sure."

"You going to run?" I asked him.

"Yeah; one day."

"Don't try it," I said.

"I ain't go'n put up with this, Jim. I wasn't cut out for it."

"Nobody was," I said. "He wasn't either."

"Him?" Marcus said, dropping the fork in his plate and looking at me like he wanted to come over there at me. "Him?" he said.

"Him," I said.

Marcus still wanted to come across that table at me, but tired and bruised as he was he knew he would have got the worst of it.

"I don't know 'bout you, Jim," he said. "You ain't no whitemouth—I don't think so—but I don't know 'bout you."

"I know," I said. "You better finish eating there and take yourself a good bath and get yourself some rest. Tomorrow is another day, and it won't be any better."

46

# 10

After I had washed the dishes, I got my guitar from against the wall and went out on the gallery. It was pitch-black out there. The moon had risen but it was still behind the trees. Somebody passed by the gate, going toward the church. I looked up the quarter and I could see the light in the four church windows. Prayer meeting was going on now. It had been going on about a month and it probably would go on another month. The last I heard, they had five candidates for baptism.

I sat on the steps and started playing my guitar. I thought about Billie Jean and played softly at first, then I tried to forget her and played something fast and hard. But I thought about her again and went back to the soft thing, then I tried to forget her and went back on the hard. After a while Jobbo came up there with his harp. Jobbo lived on the place and he was very good with a harp. He should have gone up North and made his living blowing harp, but he was the kind of nigger who was born to live and die in the South.

Marcus came out there and sat down with us. He had bathed and changed clothes, and now he looked a little better.

"Play?" I said.

"Little bit," he said.

"Want try it?"

"With these hands?"

"Hands messed up, hunh?" Jobbo said.

"Yeah," Marcus said.

"Soak them in some warm salt water," Jobbo said.

"I did that."

"They be okay in a week."

"Man, this place is black," Marcus said. "Good Lord."

"Yeah, it's pretty black, all right," Jobbo said, looking around like he hadn't seen it dark like this before.

"That's a church up there?" Marcus asked.

"Yeah, that's one," Jobbo said.

"Got any single women hanging round up there?"

"Couple, I guess," Jobbo said.

"I mean selling pussy?" Marcus said.

"That, I don't know," Jobbo said.

"Think I'll go up there," Marcus said.

"Again, huh?" I said.

"That hot bath," Marcus said. "Always happen when I take a hot bath. Can't keep this thing down."

We watched him go out of the yard. After he turned from the gate we couldn't see him any more for the picket fence.

"Trying to kill hisself, huh?" Jobbo said.

"Bonbon won't let that happen," I said.

"No, Bonbon go'n keep him 'live a while," Jobbo said. "You know, they buried that other boy today."

"Did they?"

"Yeah, they buried him. Jack Claiborn went to Port Allen. Said he heard people talking 'bout it. I feel sorry for people like Marcus."

"He doesn't," I said.

"I can see that," Jobbo said. "It don't mean a thing to him."

Just about then we saw the car lights coming down the quarter. When it went by the gate we saw it wasn't a car, it was Bonbon in the truck. He was going down to Pauline.

"Guess he need little piece tonight, too," Jobbo said.

"Guess so," I said.

"Guess what?" Jobbo said.

"What?"

"Bonbon wife looked at Bo today."

"Bonbon's wife's been looking at niggers ever since I've been here," I said.

"Look at you, too?"

"Ain't she looked at you?"

"Yeah, but I ain't crazy," Jobbo said. "But that might be some pretty good little old stuff, though."

"Try it any time you want to," I told him.

"No, thanks," Jobbo said. "I ain't ready to die yet."

I thought about Bonbon's little yellow-head wife sitting on that gallery looking up every time somebody went by the gate. I tried to vision what it would be like to bounce between those little skinny thighs. I tried to vision what it would be like to even see her smiling. I had been on that plantation over three years and all that time I had never seen her smile once. I had never heard her say anything either—but Aunt Margaret, who worked up there for them, did say she knew how to talk. Aunt Margaret said she would say something softly to her every now and then; or something to little Tite Bonbon, her little girl, every now and then; or something to Bonbon when he was there. But that wasn't too often. Because when Bonbon wasn't in the field or hunting in the woods, he was either in Bayonne selling something he had stole from Marshall Hebert or he was down the quarter in Pauline's bed. So she never said too much to him. And I guess that's why she never said too much to anyone else either. She just sat there on that gallery and looked at you when you went by, like she wished you would come in there, like she was waiting for you to try.

"Let's get *Key to the Highway*," I said.

I started plucking it real slow and sad, because now I had forgot about Bonbon or Pauline or Bonbon's little suffering wife. I was thinking about my own baby now and I wondered where she was and what she was doing. Jobbo picked up the tune after I had gone a couple bars, and if there's any man can play a sad tune sadder than Jobbo, Lord knows, I never heard him. We went on like that a few minutes—me sad, Jobbo sadder—then I told Jobbo to stop. I couldn't take it any more.

"Let's get something fast and hard, Jobbo," I said.

"Right," Jobbo said. Then he started tapping his feet and popping his fingers, going "One, two, three, four; one, two, three, four . . ."

# 11

For the first couple hours in the field the next day, Marcus could hardly straighten his back. He wore a pair of my khaki pants and shirt and the old straw hat I had tried to give him the day before. Since I was bigger than he was, my clothes didn't help his looks at all. And John and Freddie pitching that corn like they wanted to finish it all in one day wasn't helping him out either.

Bonbon showed up an hour earlier than he had done the first day and set the horse right behind Marcus. Marcus kept up with the tractor for a row, then he had to get his sack. He pulled it on the left shoulder because the right shoulder was still sore. Bonbon noticed it but didn't say anything. He just leaned a little on the pommel of the saddle and squinted his eyes from the hot sun.

It went on like that for the rest of the week. That white sun didn't let up any. John and Freddie didn't let up once, and Bonbon, neither. For my part, I couldn't do a thing but keep the tractor going at the right speed. I spoke to the Old Man a couple of times, but I'm sure He didn't hear a word I said. He had quit listening to man a million years ago. Now all He does is play chess by Himself or sit around playing solitary with old cards.

So man has to do it for himself now. No, he's not going to win, he can't ever win; but if he struggle hard and long enough he can ease his pains a little. I mean he can spread it out more and it won't hurt so much all at once. This is what Marcus did by trying to keep closer to John and Freddie. He didn't keep up all the way—no, that wasn't possible; but he did stay a little closer. Every night when he came in, he bathed his hands in salt water to draw out the soreness. By the end of the week his hands and his shoulders had gotten much better.

But wait, wait, I'm getting a little ahead of myself. I jumped to the weekend when I should have stopped at Thursday—because Thursday at twelve o'clock, Marcus saw Pauline Guerin for the first time. He was riding on the tractor beside me—not in the trailer where he had been all those other times—but standing beside me now. He was telling me about the boy he had killed. He said it was over a woman. It happened at a nightclub. The nightclub was packed and hot. There were women everywhere—women, women, and more women. But he saw only one. She had on a red dress—no, not red; sort of wine color. Everywhere she turned he was looking at her. She had the prettiest brown skin he had ever seen. He wanted her, he didn't care what it cost him, he wanted her. Every chance he got, he got in her way. Finally she noticed him and gave him a smile. Soon they were dancing and he was giving her a pile of his jive talk. He almost had her outside the door when all of a sudden somebody jerked him around and knocked him down on the floor. He looked up and he saw the same nigger he had won a pile of money from in the toilet that night. Oh yes, he said, he had forgot to tell me he had been gambling all evening and he had won a pile of money. Well, the same nigger he had won all that money from owned the woman he was trying to get outside. The same black sonofabitch—and he had a punch like a mule. When he fell he heard the nigger (they called the nigger Hotwater) telling his other nigger buddies to drag his ass outside. Before he could get to his feet, two of Hotwater's boys had him by the ankles, and the next thing he knew he was out there on his back looking at that yellow light over the door. He jumped up and he really wanted to run, but there was nowhere for him to go. The people had made a big circle round him and Hotwater, and, he said, that big, sweaty nigger wanted just one thing—his ass. He kept backing away, backing away, and that big nigger kept coming on him. Every time the nigger hit him he went down. After a while he got tired falling and he stood up and started hitting back. He said the nigger was strong and could hit like a mule, but he didn't know anything about covering up. The nigger kept his face unguarded, and he kept his fist in the nigger's face like you keep your fist on one of those little punching bags. His left cut the nigger's face so much it looked like beef liver. "You know how beef liver look?" he asked me. "Kind of blackish red?" "Yes," I said. "I know how it looks." "Well, that's how I had the nigger's face," he said. "Reddish black. The red was his blood, the black was his face." So when the nigger saw he couldn't get his face from off his fist, the nigger wanted to change tactics, Marcus said. Now he wanted his knife. But by the time the nigger got out his knife, he had got out his own, too. He said he let the nigger get two good whacks at him (he always believed in playing fair, himself); then he threw that knife into the nigger's belly far as he could. He said his hand was red when it came back. But by then the police was there, dragging him to the car.

"They was probably there all the time," he said. "But they just wanted to see one nigger kill another one. What they care."

"And soon as they threw you in jail, you sent word to your nan-nan, huh?"

"Yeah."

"And she came to Marshall Hebert?"

"That's right," he said. "I wasn't going to spend no five years in Angola for a chickenshit nigger like that. If he had o' fit me fair he wouldn't 'a' been dead."

"And that's all it means?" I asked.

"That's all it means," he said.

Just about then, we saw Pauline Guerin coming down the quarter.

# 12

Pauline wore a pink, flowery dress and a big white straw hat. She was walking slow—she always walked slow with her head high like she's always thinking about something far away. As we came closer to her she smiled and waved at us. The next moment you couldn't see her for the dust.

"Who was that?" Marcus said.

"Pauline," I said.

"I ain't never seen her before."

"She lives down there."

"She pretty," Marcus said. "That other woman was something like that. But she darker than that other woman was. She married?"

"No, but you can say she is. She's Bonbon's woman."

"Bonbon?"

"Bonbon," I said.

"Well, that sure don't cut no ice with me," he said.

"It better," I said. "It cut ice with everybody else in the quarter."

"Well, not with this kid," he said.

By then we were passing Bonbon's house, and as I glanced toward the house I saw his wife Louise sitting on the gallery in the rocking chair. She was looking at Marcus. Marcus wasn't standing more than two feet away from me, and Louise Bonbon was a good hundred and fifty feet away from the road, but I could tell she was looking only at Marcus.

"Ain't that his wife?" Marcus was saying. He hadn't noticed the look; he probably hadn't seen her looking.

"That's his wife," I said.

"So he got two, huh? A black one down the quarter and a white one up here?"

"That's about the size of it."

"And y'all don't do a thing, don't even chunk on his house at night?"

"No, we don't chunk on his house," I said. "We were waiting for you to lead us."

"I'll tell you what I'm go'n do," he said. "I'm taking that black woman."

"Sure," I said.

He jumped down and opened the gate for me, and after I had parked the two trailers before the crib, I put some water and fuel in the tractor and hooked up the empty ones. Then we went on back down the quarter.

Louise Bonbon was still on the gallery, still watching Marcus. I had seen her look at other black men in the quarter, but I had never seen her watch any like she was watching Marcus now. But Marcus wasn't paying her any attention. He was thinking about Pauline. That evening he fell back again and he had to drag that sack on his shoulder again, and that black stallion was only about six inches behind him. But he didn't mind at all. He was thinking about Pauline. He was thinking about the sweet words he was going to whisper in her ear. (He had told me what a great lover he was at dinner before we went back in the field. He had told me how once he got after a woman she couldn't do a thing

56

but fall for him.) Marcus was a pretty handsome fellow and he knew it. He was about six feet tall, slim, but well-built; he had medium brown skin and a pile of curly black hair. He had light brown eyes, a kind of straight nose, thin lips, and a well-shaped mustache. Marcus had a lot of Indian blood in him, and he probably had a lot of white blood in him, too. So already he was thinking about him and Pauline in bed. He had already seen those long, pretty arms round his neck, he had already heard the deep sighs from her throat. And after it was over, he was going to lay beside her and whisper words she had never heard before. He was going to tell her things Bonbon had never thought about. How could a white man—no, not even a solid white man, but a bayou, catfish-eating Cajun—compete with him when it came down to loving. So now he was glad Bonbon was there on the horse. He was glad the horse was so close he could feel his hot breath on the back of his neck. He was glad he could hear the *sagg-sagg-sagg* of the saddle every time the horse moved up. And even that hot, salty sweat running into his eyes couldn't make him hate Bonbon.

That night when I came back from the yard, Marcus had already taken his bath, had already ate, and had dressed.

"Taking off?" I said.

"Going courting," he said.

"Courting?"

"Miss Guerin."

"Pauline?" I said, stopping him.

"Uh-huh."

"Don't go there, Marcus," I said.

"Take it easy, babyboy, I won't hurt your overseer."

"Don't go there, Marcus," I said.

"I'm going," he said.

My grip tightened on his arm.

57

"Don't go there, Marcus," I said.

But he just stood there grinning at me.

"You want him to kill you, don't you?"

"He ain't go'n kill me, you know that."

"Don't push your luck, Marcus," I said.

"See you later, babyboy," he said, pulling my hand away from his arm and going down the steps.

# 13

Aunt Ca'line and Pa Bully lived in the same house Pauline lived in, but in opposite sides. So it was Aunt Ca'line who told me what happened. She said she and Pa Bully were sitting out on the gallery that night, and Pauline and Tick-Tock were sitting on the gallery on Pauline's side. Pauline sat in a chair by the door, and Tick-Tock, who had just come there a few minutes before, was sitting on the end of the gallery with her back against a post. There were mosquitoes that night. Aunt Ca'line was fanning them away with a piece of white rag (her special mosquito rag) and Pa Bully was using his old felt hat. Pauline had a white rag, too (maybe a diaper), and Tick-Tock had a piece of pasteboard. Every now and then Aunt Ca'line could hear the pasteboard hit against Tick-Tock's leg or her arm.

The second bell had rung for church, and Aunt Ca'line could see people passing by the gate on their way to prayer meeting. She tried to remember the last time she had been to church. She even mentioned it to Pa Bully. (She didn't call him Pa Bully, she called him Mr. Grant. And he called her Miss Caroline instead of Aunt Ca'line like the rest of us did.) She told him old as they were they ought to be in church. They were going to die soon, she said, and it wouldn't look right for people to sing and pray over them in their coffins when they hadn't been to church in so long a time. "You right there," Pa Bully said. "Yes. Yes." But even when he was saying it, Aunt Ca'line knew Pa Bully wasn't going into any church. He hadn't been inside of a church in twenty-some years.

Aunt Ca'line had been listening to the singing in the church only a few minutes when she saw somebody coming up the walk. She didn't know who it was until he spoke.

"Miss Pauline Guerin live here?" he said.

Aunt Ca'line looked at Marcus but didn't answer him. Pauline heard him asking about her but she didn't even turn her head. It was quiet for nearly a minute. Tick-Tock slapped at a mosquito on her arm, then it was quiet for nearly another minute. Marcus still hadn't moved. Aunt Ca'line said it looked like he wasn't going to ever move, so she motioned toward Pauline across the way.

Marcus started up the steps and went back down. Aunt Ca'line and Pa Bully had this barb-wire fence that came up on the gallery all the way to the wall. The fence was brought up there, according to Aunt Ca'line, to keep Pauline and Bonbon's two little mischievous mulattoes on their side. But putting the barb-wire fence up there was like putting nothing there. The two little boys had ridden the fence so much, a grown person could step over it without touching a strain of wire.

But one look at the fence, and Marcus changed his mind and went back out the yard. A second later Aunt Ca'line saw him coming back up Pauline's walk.

"Miss Guerin," he said.

Pauline didn't speak and Marcus sat on the steps. It got quiet again. Every now and then Aunt Ca'line would swing her mosquito rag at a mosquito singing round her ear. Pa

Bully had put away his hat for his pipe now, and Aunt Ca'line could hear the soft sucking on the cob pipe and then see a little stream of smoke every time Pa Bully heard or even felt a mosquito might be heading his way.

"Mr. Grant," Aunt Ca'line said, warningly.

Because, according to Aunt Ca'line, she had caught Pa Bully cutting his eyes toward the other side of that fence where they had no business going.

# 14

Aunt Ca'line had been saying "Mr. Grant" warningly like that ever since the other one first started coming to the house: that was seven or eight years ago. The other one had never sat out on the gallery. He didn't have to, because it had started long before he came there. It had started in the field, where he had all the right to call her over into a patch of corn or cotton or cane or the ditch—the one he was closest to—and make her lay down and pull up her dress. Then after he had satisfied his lust, he would get back on the horse like nothing had happened. And she would pull down her dress and go back to the work she was doing before he had called her to him. The other women wouldn't say anything to her, and she wouldn't say anything, either—like nothing in the world had happened.

But something had happened to Bonbon. At first he had laid with all and any of them. When his lust was up he had called the one closest to him. But after being with so many, now he settled for one. And when she saw what had happened, she saw her chance to make life a little sweeter.

"I'm tired of this field," she told him. "I want get in that house. I'll cook, I'll be his maid, but I'm tired of this field."

Bonbon told Marshall Hebert he was bringing her there.

Marshall Hebert couldn't say anything because Bonbon already knew something about Marshall's past. Marshall told him to bring her; then he tried to break the news to Miss Julie Rand gently as possible. But, according to Aunt Ca'line, he could have saved his breath because Miss Julie had expected that this was coming all the time.

When Pauline came to the big house she quit wearing the gingham dresses she had worn in the field. Now she wore light-color dresses that had printed flowers on them. She bought two big white straw hats—one had a red ribbon and one had a green ribbon round the band. She wore loafers and not the hard work shoes the other women wore in the field. But only Pauline's clothes had changed; she stayed pretty much the same person. From what I heard and knew about her she had always been very quiet. She was kind to everyone and had a lot of respect for the old people on the plantation. She didn't go to church but nobody had ever heard her saying anything against it. When she first started working at the big house a lot of people in the quarter felt the same way she did: they knew that long as she lived on the plantation she would have to lay with Bonbon if he wanted her to. So why not make the best of it? Why not get out of the hot sun? Why not wear better clothes, why not eat better food? Then there were the other people in the quarter who pretended she was sinning more than any of them had ever done. They did all they could to hurt her, but she took all their insults with a little smile that said, "If he had chose you, where would you be right now?"

It wasn't too long after Pauline went to the big house that Aunt Ca'line started warning Pa Bully about his eyes and his tongue. She would never say, "Mind your own business"; she would never say, "Bring your eyes back where they belong" or "Stop up your ears." She would say only two words,

"Mr. Grant"; and Pa Bully understood exactly what those two words meant. It had started the first night that Bonbon came to the house. It was summer just like it was now, and he had tied the horse at the gate and walked toward the house just like it was his own. He had not said anything to Aunt Ca'line or Pa Bully; he had said something softly to Pauline, who had been sitting in a chair by the door, and she had followed him inside. They had talked a few minutes, then they had gotten on the bed. Anybody who ever slept on a cornshuck mattress don't have to be told the noise one can make, Aunt Ca'line said. And Pauline's moaning round there didn't pacify matters at all.

"Good Lord," Pa Bully said. "What the world he got there?"

"Mr. Grant," Aunt Ca'line said, warningly.

After a while Bonbon came out and got on the horse and rode away, and a few minutes later Pauline came back on the gallery. Aunt Ca'line and Pa Bully pretended they hadn't been listening to anything. Farther up the quarter the people were singing in the church.

"Ain't that Cobb doing the leading?" Pa Bully asked Aunt Ca'line.

"Sounds like his voice," Aunt Ca'line said. She listened to the singing a while. "That's Cobb," she said. "Who else got a heavy voice like that."

# 15

Less than a year after that night, Pauline had twins. But she still wasn't in love with Bonbon. If he had walked out on her anytime, she would have gone with somebody else who would have been very glad to have her. Not because she had once belonged to this white man, but because she was still as decent as any other black woman on the place could be around him. But he didn't walk out on her, he came to her more regularly now. He didn't pick up the twins and bounce them on his knees like he would do his little girl later, but he did bring them food and clothes. He gave them toys at Christmas and he gave them pennies on Saturday to put in Sunday School. No, he didn't give the money to the children, he gave it to Pauline to give to them. Because he and the twins could never have any close-ness at all. They could never call him papa no matter how many times they heard him in the bed with mama. They couldn't even carry his name. They were called Guerin like their mother. Billy and Willy Guerin—and they were probably the worst two Billy and Willy the Good Lord had suffered for.

Bonbon was in love with Pauline when he brought her to the big house, but it took years for Pauline to fall in love with Bonbon. She didn't want to fall in love with this white man because she knew nothing good could come of it. She knew she would have to be his woman long as she lived on the plantation and long as he wanted her, but she didn't want to hold any feeling for him at all. She wanted it to be "come and go" and nothing else. She figured that after a while it would come to an end, anyhow.

But it didn't come to an end. Aunt Ca'line said Bonbon didn't miss coming there a week after he started. He came summer and winter. When the weather was good he usually came in the truck. When it had rained he would come on the horse because the truck would get stalled in the mud. Many times he got wet coming down the quarter and he would have to change his clothes at the fireplace and wrap a blanket round him while Pauline dried the clothes on the back of a chair.

After so many years, Pauline did fall in love with Bonbon. She couldn't help but fall in love with him. She knew he loved her more than he did his wife up the quarter or his people who lived on the river.

So now the shuck mattress was quiet. There wasn't any need for all the noise, because now Bonbon and Pauline's love was much softer—more tender. Aunt Ca'line and Pa Bully could hardly hear the mattress at all from their room. The twins sleeping on their bed in the kitchen probably couldn't hear the mattress either.

But this was not the only place where Pauline and Bonbon went together. Sometimes it happened at the big house while they made Bishop, Marshall Hebert's butler, look out for Marshall. Bishop hated what he had to do—but what else could he do? If he had mentioned to Marshall that Bonbon had gone farther than that kitchen, Bonbon, or Marshall himself, probably would have killed him. So he kept his mouth shut. He went out on the front gallery and looked out for Marshall like Bonbon told him to do. Since he wasn't supposed to be out there unless he was cleaning up or serving someone, Bishop had to keep himself hid. There was a palm tree on the left side of the gallery and he stood behind the tree all the time he was out there. Sometimes he had to stay there an hour. If Bonbon went to sleep he would have to stay even longer.

Marshall never did catch Pauline and Bonbon, but even if he had he probably wouldn't have done anything about it. Bonbon already had something on Marshall, and long as he held this proof Marshall couldn't do a thing but go along with him no matter what he did. This went for stealing, too. Marshall knew Bonbon was stealing from him. He had seen a lantern in the crib at night; he had heard the children laughing in there while they shelled corn that Bonbon was going to sell in Bayonne the next day. Marshall had missed hogs, he had missed cows—he had even missed bales of cotton from the barn. But since he couldn't do a thing about it, he pretended that it wasn't happening.

Bonbon was a simple man and a brutal man, was the way Aunt Ca'line described him. He was brutal because he had been brought up in a brute-taught world and in brute-taught times. The big house had given him a horse and a whip (he did have a whip at first) and they had told him to ride behind the blacks in the field and get as much work out of them as he could. He did this, but he did more: he fell in love with one of the black women. He couldn't just take her like he was supposed to take her, like they had given him permission to take her—no, he had to fall in love. When the children came he loved them, too. He couldn't tell them he loved them, he wasn't allowed to tell them that. He probably never told it to Pauline, and maybe he never told it to himself. But he could feel it, and when he did he tried to show it by giving them toys and clothes. No, no, no, he never gave it to them, he gave it to Pauline to give to them. When they made five years old he gave them a BB gun to play with together. Aunt Ca'line said the moment they learned how to shoot the gun, nobody and nothing was safe on the place. If they weren't shooting at another child, they were shooting at a dog or a chicken. They put a hole in the back of Jobbo's little girl's neck, and Jobbo had to take the girl to the doctor and pay the doctor bill himself. They shot the mule that Charlie Jordan was riding and the mule threw Charlie in the ditch. While he was trying to get up, Billy and Willy kept on shooting at him. Charlie never did get back on the mule. He ran one way, the mule took off in the other direction.

Aunt Ca'line said the day after the children got the BB gun, she noticed that her number one rooster wasn't walking straight. The rooster was acting like he was drunk. He didn't know if he wanted to go left or right.

"What's wrong with that crazy chicken?" Aunt Ca'line said. "Don't tell me them two or three little hens out there done finally wored him down—Mr. Grant, catch that chicken for me," she told Pa Bully.

Pa Bully sat on the bottom step, shelling corn and dropping it on the ground. All of the other chickens ran there to pick corn—all but the rooster. He staggered left, he staggered right; he went backward, he went forward. He looked like a child walking a rail and trying to keep his balance.

"Chip, chip, chip," Pa Bully said.

Finally, the rooster staggered toward the steps. Pa Bully grabbed him under the wings.

"Both eyes gone," he said. "Had to be shooting fast to get 'em both like that."

Aunt Ca'line took the rooster to the other side to show Pauline what her children had done. Pauline and Bonbon were in the kitchen. Bonbon was standing by the window drinking coffee. Pauline sat at the table cutting okra.

"You see what them two little bastards done done my chicken?" Aunt Ca'line said to Pauline.

"Oh, Aunt Ca'line, I'm so sorry," Pauline said. "That gun ain't causing nothing but trouble," she said to Bonbon. Bonbon sipped from his coffee but didn't say anything. "I'll pay for him," Pauline said to Aunt Ca'line.

"Pay for him?" Aunt Ca'line said. "Pay for this rooster? This rooster do the work of five on this plantation, and you go'n pay for him? What you go'n do, give me five roosters?"

"I'm sorry, Aunt Ca'line," Pauline said.

"You can be sorry if you want," Aunt Ca'line said, shaking the rooster in front of Pauline's face. "If I catch either one of them little mulatto bastards on my side again I'm go'n poison him. You hear me? I'm go'n poison the little shit."

Bonbon never said anything. He didn't even look at Aunt Ca'line. He just stood there sipping his coffee.

Aunt Ca'line didn't poison Billy or Willy, she just had the barb-wire fence brought up on the gallery. But that didn't do any good, either. The children got on the fence and rode it the way you ride a horse. The stickers on the fence didn't bother them at all. Aunt Ca'line tried to get Marshall Hebert to run electricity through the fence, but Marshall told her that was against the law.

"Ain't shooting out people chicken eye 'gainst the law?" she asked Marshall. "Ain't making mules throw old people in the ditch 'gainst the law, too?"

"Yes," Marshall said. "But I guess we'll have to put up with it."

"How long?" Aunt Ca'line asked.

"I don't know," Marshall said. "Maybe one day Bonbon'll get generous and buy them two shotguns. Maybe they'll load them and shoot at each other at the same time."

Aunt Ca'line and everybody else on the place waited for Bonbon to buy the two shotguns. He never did.

# 16

They'd been sitting on the gallery half an hour and no-body had said a thing. Every now and then Aunt Ca'line swung her mosquito rag just in case a mosquito was headed that way. At the same time she could hear Pa Bully sucking on the pipe and blowing out a stream of smoke just in case the mosquito changed his mind about biting her and decided to get him. Aunt Ca'line wasn't looking toward the other end of the gallery any more so she didn't know what Pauline was doing. But Tick-Tock was still slapping at mosquitoes with the pasteboard, and every now and then Marcus would hit at one on his arm or his face.

Things were so quiet on the gallery, Aunt Ca'line could hear all the singing and praying in the church. She was thinking how she and Pa Bully ought to get back in the church again. She wondered what the people would think if she walked into church Sunday morning and told them she wanted to pick up the Cross. She was thinking about this seriously when all of a sudden one of Pauline's little boys bust into the yard.

"Now, what?" Aunt Ca'line asked herself. "What—where is that other one?" (The little boy busting into the yard had made her forget about church.) "When you see one, you see two, now where is that other one? Where—" Then she saw the dust. She didn't see the boy—he was running too fast; she saw the dust trailing him up the quarter. "Now what they done done?" she asked herself. "Whose pig they been riding this time?"

Then she started thinking about the teacher. The teacher had gone around with the shakes two weeks before he broke down and ran away from Hebert's plantation. And the reason was this: The teacher had whipped one of the little boys for hitting Jobbo's little girl. He didn't see which one had hit the little girl and the little girl wasn't too sure, either, but she said she thought it was Billy. Billy said it wasn't him, it was Willy. Willy said no, it wasn't him, it was Billy. So the teacher said, "Come here, Billy," and whipped Billy. Then Willy said it wasn't Billy, it was him, Willy. Then Billy said he was going to tell his paw.

The teacher said he had been living in the South long enough to know that no black child was going up to a white man and say "paw," so it wasn't this that had brought on the shakes. What scared him half to death was that one of the other children might let his mouth slip in front of Bonbon and get Bonbon to believing that he (the teacher) was allowing Billy and Willy to go around school calling him "father." Though every grownup on the place and every child at school knew that Bonbon was Billy and Willy's father, they still were not allowed to say it in public. Billy and Willy, for all everybody was supposed to know, came out of a cabbage patch. There was no father. Or if there was, he surely was not white.

So the teacher went around with the shakes for two weeks, because he knew that one of the children was going to let his mouth slip in front of Bonbon. And he knew then that Bonbon and his dozen or so brothers were going to come to the churchhouse and drag him out of there and lynch him. But after two weeks had passed and Bonbon still had not showed up, the teacher thought he had better leave because the tension was slowly killing him, anyhow.

Aunt Ca'line was thinking about the teacher when the second boy bust into the yard. Then halfway up the walk both of them threw on brakes. They came toward the gallery now so quietly, you would have thought they had never done a minute's devilment in all their lives.

"How y'all feel there, Aunt Ca'line?" they spoke to her and Pa Bully.

"So-so, and y'all?" she and Pa Bully said.

"Fine, thank you ma'am," they said at the same time.

They looked at Marcus but didn't speak to him. They spoke to Tick-Tock, then they went up on the gallery where Pauline sat by the door.

"Hi, mo' dear," they both said at the same time, both kissing her on the face at the same time.

"Y'all ain't been up to nothing, I hope," Pauline said.

"They was born up to something," Aunt Ca'line thought. "What you asking them that for?"

"No'm," they said at the same time.

"Y'all go in there and wash your hands and eat," Pauline said.

"All right, mo' dear," they said. They kissed her again. But this time the one who had kissed her on the right jaw before kissed her on the left jaw, and the one who had kissed her on the left jaw kissed her on the right one. Or so it looked to Aunt Ca'line. But who could be sure who did what? One was the other one and the other one was the same one. The only person alive who knew Billy from Willy was Pauline. Even Bonbon couldn't tell them apart.

After the twins went inside everything got quiet again.

"Think I'll make it on in," Tick-Tock said.

"Taking off, Tickey?" Pauline said.

"Yeah," Tick-Tock said. "Got to hit that cotton field again in the morning."

Tick-Tock said good night to Pauline and then to Aunt Ca'line and Pa Bully, and went out of the yard. She hadn't said anything to Marcus.

"Can I speak to you?" Marcus said, standing up and facing Pauline.

"Speak," she said.

"Somewhere by usself," he said.

"What you got to say to me, you can say it in front of Aunt Ca'line and Pa Bully."

"Come, Mr. Grant, let's go inside," Aunt Ca'line said.

"No, don't y'all leave," Pauline said. "Your name Marcus, ain't it?" she said to him.

"Yes," Marcus said.

"Say what's on your mind, Marcus."

"I want us to speak by usself," he said.

"Then you better leave," she said.

"You ain't even heard what I had to say."

"If you can't say it in front of Aunt Ca'line and Pa Bully, I don't need to hear it," she said.

"I just want come and see you sometime," he said.

"I didn't hear that," she said. "You can leave."

But he didn't move. He stood there looking at her like he wanted to come closer and touch her. Pauline wore a light green dress that had dark green leaves and red flowers. She looked fresh and pretty sitting there.

"And don't come back, please," she said. "I don't want no trouble."

"They don't have to be no trouble," Marcus said.

"No, they won't be any," she said, getting up. "Good night."

He started toward her.

"Pauline—"

Just about then the twins came into the doorway. Aunt Ca'line could see just the front of them; she didn't know if they had anything behind their backs or not.

"Y'all get back inside," Pauline said to the twins. They moved back. "Yes?" she said to Marcus.

"You the prettiest lady I know," he said.

"Thank you," she said. "Good night."

"Can I speak to you sometime?"

"I speak to everybody," she said. "Good night."

She went in. He stood there a while, then he went down the steps.

"That one won't be here long," Pa Bully said. "And on the other hand he might."

"Six feet under, you mean?" Aunt Ca'line said.

"Six feet under," Pa Bully said.

# 17

Marcus got up early the next morning and went to the yard with me to get the tractor. He thought he was going to see Pauline, but I could have told him she didn't go to work until nine o'clock. That morning in the field, John and Freddie worked him just as hard as they had done the day before and the day before that. At twelve he went up the quarter with me again, still hoping to see Pauline. He saw Louise Bonbon sitting out on the gallery, but he paid no more attention to her than he did a weed standing 'side the road. He still didn't know she was watching him. He saw her looking that way but he still didn't know it was him she was looking at. He looked for Pauline again when we came up to the yard. He didn't see her at first, but as we were getting ready to go back down the quarter he saw her coming from the store. He watched her walk across the yard.

"Jim," she said, waving at me when she came closer.

"How's it going, chicken?"

"So-so," she said. Then she looked at Marcus and nodded.

"Hot enough for you?" I said.

"Too hot," she said.

"You got it made, chicken," I said.

She smiled and went toward the house. And Marcus just

75

stood there looking at her, looking at the smooth, easy way her body moved in that dress. I knew where his mind was. It was there and nowhere else.

"Let's get to getting," I said.

We started on back down the quarter, and again I saw Louise watching him from the gallery.

That evening Bonbon was out there again. Marcus fell back and had to drag the sack on his shoulder. He still thought he was going to make Pauline, but you could see he wasn't sure as he was the day before. You could see him watching Bonbon from the side. He wondered what it was about Bonbon could make Pauline love him. He couldn't understand how Pauline could love a white man. How could she possibly love one? He still didn't want to believe she did.

He went back down there again that night. Aunt Ca'line and Pa Bully were sitting on the gallery just like the night before. Aunt Ca'line was fighting off mosquitoes with her special mosquito rag, and Pa Bully was fighting them with his hat. Pauline was sitting by the door in her chair, and Tick-Tock was sitting on the end of the gallery against the post. Aunt Ca'line and Pa Bully were talking softly to each other when she looked up and saw Marcus coming into Pauline's yard. Aunt Ca'line heard Tick-Tock saying, "Lover-boy."

Pauline didn't say anything.

Tick-Tock said, "Hope a certain party ain't coming here tonight."

"Tomorrow," Pauline said.

They watched Marcus come up the walk.

"Good evening," he said.

Nobody spoke, but Pauline nodded. Then it was quiet for a while. Farther up the quarter the people were singing in the church.

"Cobb got 'em going up there," Pa Bully said.

"Yes," that's Cobb, all right," Aunt Ca'line said.

It was quiet for about ten minutes; then everybody on the gallery saw the car lights coming down the quarter. Tick-Tock slid off the end of the gallery and nearly ran out of the yard. Nobody else moved. Since Pauline didn't look worried, Aunt Ca'line said she wasn't worried, either. Pa Bully wasn't going to move unless Aunt Ca'line moved—and Marcus acted like he wouldn't move no matter who it was.

The car didn't stop. It wasn't Bonbon, it was Marshall Hebert. Marshall went down the quarter and turned around and went back out again.

"Good night, Aunt Ca'line, you and Pa Bully," Pauline said.

"Good night," they said to her.

Pauline stood up to take her chair inside, and Marcus jumped up, too.

"Pauline?" he said.

"I told you to stay 'way from here," she told him.

"Pauline?" he said, going toward her.

"You stay 'way from my house," she told him.

"Boy, can't you hear?" Pa Bully said.

"Mr. Grant," Aunt Ca'line said, warningly.

"Pauline?" he said, still going toward her.

She went in and locked the door. Marcus stood before the door a long time before he turned around and went back down the steps.

# 18

Twelve o'clock Saturday we were through for the week, and Marcus went to the yard with me. Louise watched him from her gallery when we passed by the house but he still didn't pay her any mind.

"I didn't think you could do it," I said.

"I can do anything," he said.

"That's your trouble," I told him. "You ought to show some humbleness sometime."

"For what?" he said.

"Just so people can like you, Marcus."

"People," he said. "People the cause I'm in the trouble I'm in now."

"Not people," I said. "You put yourself in that trouble. If you hadn't messed with that woman you wouldn't have been in it."

"If that nigger hadn't been chickenshit, I wouldn't have been in it," he said.

"That was his woman," I said. "Don't you think he had the right?"

"Any man's a fool to die over a woman," he said. "They got too many of 'em."

He got down and opened the gate for me; then after I had

gone in the yard and after he had locked the gate, he got back on the tractor.

"When I get back I'm go'n take a good hot bath and just rest, rest for a while," he said.

"I'm going to rest first, then I'll take a bath," I said.

"I can't rest with dirt on me," he said.

"City boy, huh?"

"Yeah, I guess so," he said. "I like soap and water and I like cologne. You can have some if you want some. Women got to run after you with that stuff smelling."

"No, thanks," I said. "I'll stick to plain soap and water."

"Go on and be country if you want to," he said.

I drove up to the crib and parked the tractor. We had just climbed down and gone around the trailer when I saw Bonbon coming across the yard. He raised his hand with one finger sticking up. We stopped to see what he wanted.

"Made it, huh?" he said.

"Yeah."

Bonbon had on a pair of clean, well-pressed khakis. He wore his white cowboy hat and not the sweat-stained straw hat he wore in the field everyday. He had on a pair of brown shoes and not the cowboy boots he always wore when he rode the horse.

Bonbon was about six-four or -five, and I must say he was an impressive-looking man. He was handsome—I think very handsome—but nothing pretty or cute. Marcus, I think, was pretty. Young gals would say that Marcus was "dreamy." Nobody would say Bonbon was dreamy, like nobody would say he was ugly. He was handsome in a rough way. He had a good build—maybe two hundred, two hundred and ten pounds. He had light gray eyes, a long, good-shaped nose, and a dry-shuck-color mustache. His mustache was lighter than his tan face and much lighter than his red neck.

"Burning up," he said.

"Yeah, I'm going to make it on down," I said. "Paying off about the same time, huh?"

"Yeah; four, four thirty."

"I'll be back up then," I said. "Anything else you want me to do?"

"No, not you," he said.

Then I knew why he had stopped us. Marcus didn't move. "You," he said.

Marcus waited. I waited, too.

"Them children we had unloading that corn there all took sick."

Marcus didn't know what Bonbon was getting to. I did.

"That's your job this evening," he said.

"My job?" Marcus said. "Unload that? Unload all that corn? I load all that corn."

Bonbon looked across the yard. He had given his orders; he didn't think there was any need to carry it any farther.

Marcus started trembling. I could see his fist tighten and then gradually open. For a second there I thought he was going to act a fool and jump on Bonbon. But Bonbon wasn't worried at all. And I think that's what made Marcus so mad. Bonbon gave him an order and forgot all about him.

"It's hot," Bonbon said. He took off his hat and wiped his forehead with the flat side of his wrist.

Marcus looked up at Bonbon, who wasn't paying him any attention; then he leaned against the trailer and started crying. He cried so deep and fully, his whole body was shaking.

"Can he eat?" I asked Bonbon.

"Sure," Bonbon said. "Just be there at one."

"Come on," I said to Marcus. "Let's go to the store."

Marcus turned away with me.

"See you," I said to Bonbon.

"Yeah, see you there, Geam," he said.

Marcus and I didn't say anything all the way to the store. I bought a loaf of bread, a can of lunch meat, a cake, a couple big bottles of pop; then we went out on the gallery. The sun was on the gallery, so we moved to the big pecan tree to the right of the store. The pecan tree was no more than three or four feet from the highway. On the other side of the highway was the river. You had to climb through a barb-wire fence and feel your way down a steep, grassy bank before you came to the water. Right now the river was clear and blue. Later this evening when it got cool, the white people would be out there in their boats.

"You can push a man too far," Marcus said. "I worked— what more can I do?"

"You'll have off tomorrow," I said.

"Tomorrow? Tomorrow? What about today?"

Nothing I would have said could help matters so I didn't say any more. I opened the can of lunch meat, and sliced it up and put it on the bread. I gave Marcus half and I took the rest. He raised the food to his mouth, then he started trembling and threw it down.

"Lord, have mercy," he said, crying.

"You better eat," I told him.

"Eat?" he said. "Eat?" He looked like he wanted to jump on me.

"Eat," I said. I handed him another sandwich. "Here."

He wouldn't take it. The tears just rolled down his face.

"Here," I said.

He still wouldn't take it—just looking at me with the tears rolling down his face.

"Marcus?" I said.

He drew back and knocked the food out of my hand. The bread went one way, the meat went the other way.

"All right," I said. "I did all I could."

I went back to eating. When I finished I stood up.

"I'll see you," I said.

"I got to do all that by myself?" he said.

"You killed that boy by yourself, Marcus," I said.

"It's not for that boy," he said.

"No," I said. "It's not for the boy. But you killed him; that's why you're here."

I went on down the quarter. It must have been a good hundred. That dust was white as snow, hot as fire. The sun was straight up, so it didn't throw any kind of shadows across the road. You had not\_\_\_\_\_ but hot dust to walk in from the time you left the highway until you got home.

# 19

After I took a bath and a nap I went back to the front to get paid. Marshall Hebert was paying off on the store gallery. He always paid off out there when it was hot. When it was cold or raining he paid off inside the store. Marshall was sitting behind a little gray table with the roll book and the money on the table in front of him. He had stacks of twenty-dollar bills, tens, fives, and ones; in change he had halves, quarters, nickels, and pennies. Marshall was a big man with a red face and light blue eyes. He was a heavy drinker and even now he looked half drunk. Winter and summer he wore a seersucker suit and a panama hat. His coat and hat hung on the back of the chair now. His shirt collar was opened and his shirt was soaking wet with sweat.

The line of people waiting to get paid stretched from the end of the gallery almost to the mouth of the quarter. It was about four o'clock, but it was still blazing hot. Everybody was fanning. The women used their straw hats and pieces of pasteboard. The men used their hats or pocket handker-chiefs. The handkerchiefs were wet and dirty because the men had been wiping their faces with them, too. Bonbon, who stood on the gallery 'side Marshall, was the only person who looked cool. His khaki shirt was just as neat and dry as it was when I saw him at twelve o'clock. No doubt he had been sitting near the electric fan inside the store. Now he was standing there drinking a Coke. He spoke to everybody who came up to the end of the gallery to get paid. The people nodded or spoke, then they went inside the store or back down the quarter. Some of them stood on the side of the road trying to get a ride into town. By the time I came up to the gallery to get paid, Bonbon had finished his Coke and was standing there with the empty bottle in his hand. I spoke to him, then I spoke to Marshall. Marshall didn't speak. He looked too tired to speak. It wasn't just the heat, either; he was like this summer and winter. I think every day of his life was nothing but a burden for him to carry. After checking the roll book he reached me my money. I thanked him and stepped to the side.

"Don't give it all to the first gal you meet," Bonbon said to me.

"I won't," I said. "Is it all right if I take Marcus a Coke?"

"Go on."

When I mentioned Marcus's name, I saw Marshall looking at me. I went in and bought the Coke, then I came back out and walked down the quarter to the big gate. If I could have gone through the back of the store I could have saved myself plenty time and walking. But a colored person couldn't go through the back of the store to the yard. He had to enter the yard from the big gate. Only white people or servants who worked inside the house could come in from the store.

When I came up to the crib, Marcus had just about finished unloading the first trailer. He looked so beat and sweaty, I didn't see how he was going to get the second trailer done.

"How's it going?" I asked him.

Marcus looked down at me with an armful of corn. Right now he hated me as much as he hated Bonbon or Marshall.

"I brought you a Coke," I said.

Marcus pitched the armful of corn into the crib. I opened the bottle with my knife and raised it up to him. He threw some more corn into the crib before he reached down and took the bottle from me.

"Making good time," I said. "Few more hours and you'll have it all done."

Marcus drank his Coke and didn't say anything. His khaki shirt was soaking wet with sweat. Sweat ran from both of his temples down the side of his face.

"Going to Bayonne," I said. "Need anything?"

He still wouldn't answer.

"After you unload this one," I said, "all you have to do is move the tractor up a little."

Marcus raised the bottle to his mouth and looked across the yard. He didn't even look at me any more.

I walked away from the trailer. I was going to Bayonne with Snuke Johnson, Burl Colar and Jack Claiborn. They were waiting for me in Snuke's car when I came out the yard. Bayonne was ten, twelve miles away, and we made it there in about twenty minutes. After I bought a shirt uptown, we went back of town and had a few drinks. Jack Claiborn saw one of his old girlfriends and she invited us over to her place. When we got there she called three more of her friends over. The one I was talking to was sort of short and a little plump, and after a while we went in the bedroom. She pretended I was the best she ever had and I told her she was the best I ever had. When I got up she asked me for two dollars more than what she had asked me for at first.

"Sure," I said, and threw it on the dresser.

"Now, you mad," she said.

"No, I'm not mad," I said, getting into my pants.

"Don't do that," she said, still laying there. "Come back here."

"I don't have seven more to give you," I said.

"Don't talk like that," she said. "Come back here."

I sat on the bed and looked down at her. My pants was down round my ankles. She started messing with the hairs round my navel. I pushed my pants off and got back in bed with her again.

"That's the way the world is, Honey Dew, you know that?" she said.

"Sure," I said.

"That's the way it is. You get what you can."

"Sure," I said.

"But mama ain't like the rest of these old people round here," she said. "Mama go'n give her Honey Dew little dessert."

"How much?" I said.

"Don't talk like that," she said. "Just steaks and no dessert ain't good for no man. 'Specially mama's Honey Dew."

After it was over I got up and looked down at her. She was kind of pretty with her plump, big-eyes self. I took out five more and laid it on the dresser. She shook her head.

"You don't have to do that."

I went back to the bed and kissed her on both of her sweet, soft goodness. She put her arms round my neck and kissed me hard on the mouth. Then she got up and put on her clothes. After she picked up all her money, we went out.

I looked at Snuke Johnson and he was looking worried.

"What's the matter?" I said.

"We got to get back," he said. "I got to take Josie them three cases of beer for the fair."

"Fuck Josie," Burl said.

Jack Claiborn laughed. "You fuck her. I want Ethel."

"You going or I'm going?" Burl asked.

"You go," Jack said. "You pulled the first trey."

"Come here, woman, let me give you li'l satisfaction," Burl said to the woman he had been talking to.

So Burl went in and stayed about an hour, and all that time Snuke Johnson was looking worried. Then Jack went in and stayed his hour and Snuke Johnson was looking even more worried. When Jack came out everybody was waiting for Snuke to go in. Everybody could see how bad Snuke's little yellow, bad hair woman wanted to go in. Then Snuke got up and went in with her, but about fifteen minutes later they came out. In all my days I've never seen a more hurting look on anybody's face like I saw on Snuke Johnson's woman's face when she came out of that room. Most women try to hide it when things don't go well, but Snuke's woman didn't care if the whole world knew.

It was about nine when we left the women, and by the time we got the beer from the store and got back to the quarter it was close to ten. Snuke was bitching all the way back. He said he knew Josie was going to be mad. But it wasn't his fault, he said. He said Burl, Jack and I were to blame.

When we passed the big gate, I looked over the yard and I saw a lantern hanging outside the crib. So Marcus was still there.

"What's Bonbon trying to do, kill him off in one week?" Jack Claiborn asked.

"Trying to break him," I said.

"He'll do it, too," Jack said.

"I wouldn't bet on it," I said.

# 20

The quarter has two house fairs every Saturday night. Mrs. Laura Mae gives one up the quarter and Josie Henderson gives one down the quarter. Mrs. Laura Mae's fair is quiet and orderly. She doesn't have any music, and only good people—usually Christians—go there. Her food is better than Josie's food—her pralines, her cookies, her gumbo—and I think she even gives you more for your money. Still, most of the people go to Josie's fair because Josie's got music. She's even got an old loud-speaker hung up on the gallery so you can hear the music all over the plantation. Josie's got another room for gambling, and still another room with a bed for—well, you can guess for what. Josie is the only single person on the plantation, woman or man, who's got a whole house to herself. According to the people in the quarter, Bonbon had something to do with that, too. He was getting a cut out of everything Josie was bringing in.

Just like any other night, the quarter was pitch-black. And in that blackness we could hear the music coming from Josie's house fair. That old loud-speaker was all worn out and that music had a gritty sound, but still it brought the people there.

When we got down to Josie's, the place was crowded,

noisy and hot. Everybody in the front was dancing. Snuke, Jack Claiborn, and I had the beer. Burl didn't have anything; he was walking behind Jack. Josie was in the kitchen when we first came in, but before we got halfway across the room she was in there where we were. Josie was short and stocky and she was strong as a man. She could curse like hell, too. She pushed her way toward us, looking straight at Snuke Johnson. She was sweating and you could see she was mad. I thought Snuke was going to drop that case of beer and run.

"That beer better be cold," Josie said.

"No, it's—"

Josie started trembling like she wanted to hit Snuke with her fist. I could see her mouth trembling.

"You rotten sonofabitch," she said. "You rotten—where the hell you been, Snuke Johnson?"

"I didn't know—"

"You just a lying sonofabitch," Josie said. She still wanted to hit him with her fist. "I told you I was low on beer. I told you I wanted that beer back before sundown. I told you that."

"I'm—"

Then she moved closer to Snuke Johnson and started sniffing. She was sniffing like a dog on a hot trail—going, "Sniff, sniff, sniff."

"What's that I smell?" she said. But she didn't wait for Snuke to answer. She moved right up to me and started sniffing, then she moved right up to Jack and started sniffing at him. She looked at Burl but she didn't go to him; she went back to Snuke.

"So that's it," she said. "That's why you couldn't get back—"

"I don't know what you talking 'bout," Snuke said. "You ain't smelling no more than that gumbo—"

"What you say?" she said real quickly. She wanted to hit Snuke so bad she was trembling. I supposed the only reason she didn't hit him, she didn't want him dropping that case of beer. "What you say, Snuke Johnson? What you say?" she said.

"Nothing," Snuke said. Snuke was sweating now.

"Yeah, you said something," Josie said. "What you say 'bout my food?"

Snuke didn't answer her. She stood there looking at him, still trembling. Her mouth was trembling.

"Give me that goddamn beer here," she said, jerking the case out of Snuke's hands and rattling the bottles. "You can go back and find that whore again if you want. You, you put that case on here," she said to me.

"I'll take it in the kitchen, Josie," I said.

"Put it on here," she said.

"I'll take it for you, Josie."

"Put it on here," she hollered at me.

"All right," I said, setting it on the other case in her hands. She went to Jack Claiborn.

"Give me that case of beer," she said.

"Go on, Josie," Jack said. "You got 'nough. You want a rupture?"

"Put that goddamn beer on here," she said, "before I set the rest of these cases down and kick your ass."

"Here," Jack said, dropping the case real hard on the others.

Josie turned with the three cases of beer and staggered a little, but she was able to make it back into the kitchen. I went back there a couple minutes later. The kitchen was blazing hot. You could smell nothing but fried fish and gumbo back there. Josie was on her knees, putting the last few bottles of beer in a tub of ice. I offered to help her but she wouldn't let me. So I went over to the window to stand in the fresh air.

"I woulda thought you knowed better," she said. "You starting to act just like the rest of them round here."

"It probably slipped his mind, Josie," I said. "You ran completely out?"

"I been out since eight o'clock and people been begging and begging for beer," Josie said. "I told him I was go'n run out. I told him hurry back. Hell, if he didn't want do it he ought to been said it."

"He just forgot, Josie," I said.

"Forgot hell," she said, getting up off her knees. "I can smell him a mile. You, too."

"All right," I said. "How about some gumbo. And how about a beer—a Coke to go with it."

Josie was near the stove when I mentioned the word "beer." She stopped and looked at me, trembling a little.

"Don't play with me, no, James," she said. "Don't play with me now."

"I'm sorry, Josie," I said. "I meant Coke."

"I'm warning you," she said, still trembling a little. "I ain't in no playing mood."

"I'm sorry, Josie," I said.

She went on and dished me up a big bowl of gumbo and rice, and I stood at the window, eating. The gumbo was so hot with pepper it set the roots of your hair on fire. I drank two bottles of Coke, but the Coke didn't do any good. It made that gumbo even hotter.

When I got through eating I paid Josie and went in the front room where everybody was dancing. But it was too crowded in there and I pushed my way in the other room where the gambling was going on. There must have been a dozen people in there. Jocko Thompson was the house-man.

Jocko was short, heavy-set, with a big head and real kinky hair. His white shirt was unbuttoned and you could see the kinky hairs on his sweaty chest.

Black Ned was sitting on Jocko's left side. Black Ned was black as his name. He was about twenty-five but he looked fifteen. He was one of those black people who was going to look fifteen until he was forty, then he was going to look twenty-one. Sun Brown was sitting next to Black Ned. Sun Brown wasn't brown, he was yellow. He was tall, skinny and yellow. He wore a yellow straw hat that had a red and green band that had a little red feather stuck in it. Sun always kept his cards close to his face when he was gambling. The Aguillard brothers were there, too. Two of them were sitting at the table, three more were standing around. They were the five biggest cowards in Louisiana. Together they would gang you; catch one by himself, you could make him crawl a mile. Murphy Bacheron was the other man at the table. Murphy didn't live on the plantation but he came there to gamble. Murphy was a big, barrel-chested, broad-shouldered, thick-necked, gravel-voice, derby-wearing man. He had been in so many fights, he had scars all over his face and neck. I supposed he had them all over his body, too. He was some-where between fifty and sixty, but he was as much man as anybody thirty. You couldn't make that whole Aguillard gang jump on Murphy.

"Johnson got back with that fucking beer?" Black Ned asked me.

"Yeah, but it's hot."

"Hot? What the fuck it's hot for?"

"Because it's not cold," I said.

"Yeah?" Black Ned said, nodding his head. "You think you funny, don't you, Kelly?"

"You want a card, boy?" Jocko Thompson asked him.

OF LOVE AND DUST

"Boy?" Black Ned said, looking from me to Jocko. "How
big do men grow on this fucking plantation?"

"You want a card, boy?" Jocko said, looking at him like
he hadn't even heard him.

"What kind of fucking place is this, a man can't even have
a cold beer when he's gambling? Black Ned said, ignoring
Jocko Thompson because Jocko called him a boy. He let
everybody wait on him a while before he looked at his cards.
He rapped his knuckles on the table. "Hit me," he said.

Jocko threw him a nine. That busted him. He threw his
cards on the table and cursed again.

"Hit me," Sun Brown said, real quiet-like.

Jocko Thompson threw him a four. Sun Brown brought
the cards real close to his face.

"Play these," he said.

Then he peeped around the cards at Jocko Thompson,
then he peeped over the cards at me, then he looked closely
at them again. I had to laugh to myself.

"Playing what I got," the first Aguillard boy said.

"Hit me," the other one said.

Jocko threw him a five.

"Play this," he said, after he had looked at his cards again.

"Murphy?" Jocko asked.

"Play what I got," Murphy said in his graveled voice.

"Seventeen," Sun Brown said, showing his cards.

"I got seventeen," the Aguillard boy said, showing his.

"Nineteen," the other one said, spreading his cards out.

Murphy turned over two kings and raked in the money.
He threw Jocko Thompson a quarter.

"You keep winning, don't you, Murphy?" one of the
standing Aguillard brothers said.

"Yeah," Murphy said in his graveled voice. "You think
you can change my luck?"

That was Tram who had spoke. He was the oldest; he was the leader of the gang. Murphy just sat there looking up at Tram. Murphy's shirt was unbuttoned, too, and you could see that kinky hair on that big sweaty chest like a bunch of flies on a rain-drenched pecan tree.

"That fucking beer ain't cold yet?" Black Ned said. "What the fuck Josie doing, setting on them bottles herself?"

"You want in?" Jocko Thompson asked me.

"No," I said.

"Nobody go'n bite you, Kelly," one of the sitting-down Aguillards said to me.

"I'm not scared of that, either," I said.

"Where your convict friend at?" the other one asked me. "Marcus?"

"Yeah. He the one."

"He's around," I said.

"You mean round that crib up there, don't you?"

Then all five of the Aguillards laughed. They thought it was the funniest thing they had ever heard of.

"Anybody in that back room?" Black Ned said. "A man can't have a cold beer, he might as well fuck."

"What, your fist?" one of the Aguillard brothers said.

"That's your habit?" Black Ned said to him.

"Don't get smart, boy," one of the standing Aguillards said.

Black Ned took out his little snub-nosed thirty-eight and laid it on the table.

"Put that shit back in your pocket," Jocko told him.

"Just want people round here to know I back up my word," Black Ned said, putting the gun back.

"Somebody go'n make you eat that goddamn popgun one day," one of the standing Aguillards said.

"Sure," Black Ned said. "Kelly, go get me a beer, huh."

"Get it yourself," I said. "I'm no waiter."

"Well, fuck you, nigger," he said.

"Sure," I said.

Jocko Thompson was dealing out the cards. Sun Brown was holding his close up to his face.

I stood there about half an hour, then I went out. Maybe I would get in the game later when it quieted down some, but I didn't want any part of it now.

# 21

The other room was still hot and crowded, but no matter where you turned people were dancing. The music was blaring all over the place. I stood in there a while talking to Jack Claiborn who was leaning on the mantelpiece; then I went in the kitchen. The kitchen wasn't so crowded but it was twice as hot. Josie was dishing up a bowl of gumbo for a man standing at the window.

"How's the beer?" I asked Josie.

"They been drinking it hot," she said.

"I better get one," I said.

"Get him one, Tick," Josie said to Tick-Tock.

"Get yourself one, too," I said to Tick-Tock.

Tick-Tock opened the bottles on an opener against the wall and gave me mine. It was cool but it was long ways from cold.

"Your boy Marcus got through unloading that corn," Tick-Tock said to me. "He came down the quarter few minutes ago. Jim, why don't you make him leave Pauline alone. Not that nobody go'n tell Mr. Sidney, but he might catch him hisself."

"I've talked to him already," I said, "and he won't listen. If Bonbon catch him, it'll just be his hard luck."

A few minutes later Pauline came in. She stopped in the

front room to talk a while; then as she started into the kitchen one of the Aguillard brothers came out of the other room and asked her to dance. She danced with him to a couple records, then she came on back where we were.

"Oh, it's hot," she said. She was fanning with a little white handkerchief. "Hi, Jim."

"How's it going?"

"It's burning up."

"Beer?" I said.

"I don't mind."

"Not cold."

"I'll take anything. Then I have to go. Left the children by themself."

"Let Aunt Ca'line look after them."

"Who'll look after Aunt Ca'line?" Pauline said.

I smiled at her and she smiled back. I looked at her a long time to let her know how much I liked her. But she already knew how much I liked her, and she also knew I knew that there was somebody else in her life.

I bought her another beer; then she bought two pralines for the twins and left. Tick-Tock had told her she ought to get somebody to walk home with her, but she told Tick-Tock that she had left the gallery light on and she would be all right.

Just after Pauline walked out of the house a squabble broke out in the room where the men were gambling. It sounded like somebody had overturned the gambling table. Then it sounded like somebody picked up somebody else and slammed him against the wall. There was a lot of tussling in there a while, then everybody came out. They were still arguing but nobody was throwing any punches. That is, nobody threw a punch until Marcus came in there and hit Murphy Bacheron up 'side the head.

97

But I'm getting a little ahead of myself here. I was talking about Pauline. As she went out of the yard, who should she see coming down the quarter but Marcus. I wasn't there, I didn't see it, but Aunt Ca'line and Pa Bully were still on the gallery, and Aunt Ca'line talked about it later. Josie's gallery light was on and Pauline's gallery light was on, so Aunt Ca'line could see the two people coming toward each other. They came closer and closer, and Aunt Ca'line could see how Pauline was moving toward the ditch to get out of his way. But Marcus moved there, too. Then they stopped. Pauline wanted to pass by but Marcus wouldn't let her. They were standing just outside the fence, and Aunt Ca'line could hear them talking.

"Let me pass, Marcus," Pauline was saying. "I'm telling you, now."

"What he got on you?" Marcus said. "What's the matter with you, woman?"

"I'm telling you, let me pass," Pauline said.

"What's the matter with you?" he said. "I been working up there all night like a slave, like a dog—and all on 'count of him. What's the matter with you?"

"I'm telling you," she said. "Let me pass."

He moved closer.

"Don't you put your hands on me," she said. "I mean it, don't you put your hands on me, you killer."

He hit her and knocked her down. She got up.

"If I tell him, he'll kill you for this. He'll kill you."

"You white man bitch," he said. He hit her again. She fell again.

"Leave that woman 'lone, boy," Pa Bully hollered at him.

"Mr. Grant," Aunt Ca'line said, warningly.

"You hear me out there, boy?" Pa Bully called.

Pauline was up again.

"You bitch," Marcus said to her. "You bloody whore."

She was running toward the gate now.

"You whore," he called to her.

She was running in the yard now. She ran in the house and locked the door. He stood there a while looking at the house; then he went on.

When Marcus came into Josie's house, everything stopped. Everybody stopped dancing, everybody stopped talking— they stopped everything to look at him. They hadn't heard the noise outside, but they had heard about him. And now here he was in person.

Marcus pushed his way back into the kitchen. He wore a pair of white pants and a blue silk shirt. He wore a brown plaited-cloth belt round his waist. He had on black and white shoes.

"What you know, buddy?" I said to him.

"Give me a beer," he said to Josie.

"I'm out," Josie said.

He didn't believe she was out. He thought she didn't want to sell him any.

"She's out," I said.

"What you got?" Marcus said. "Give me some whiskey. You want anything?" he asked me.

"I'll take a shot," I said.

"Give me some whiskey," he told Josie.

Josie got the bottle out of the safe and poured me and him a shot.

"Fifty cents," she said.

Marcus paid her. Then he downed his drink quickly and asked for another one.

"You want another one?" he asked me.

"No," I said. "This is good."

"Just took that for old buddy sake, huh?" he said.

"Take it easy, boy," I said.

"Fuck it," he said.

"I don't like that kind of talk in here," Josie said.

"No?" Marcus said.

"No," Josie said, looking hard at him and meaning it. And she had that bottle in her hand to back her up.

"Pour," Marcus said.

She poured. He paid her and drunk it down.

"Give me another one," he said.

"You had enough, Marcus," I said.

"Yeah?" he said. "Pour," he told Josie.

"This your last one," Josie said. "I don't want your money."

"What's the matter with my money?" he said.

"Nothing," I said. "Come on, let's—"

"Take your fucking hands off me," he said, knocking my hand away.

"All right, buddy," I said.

He downed the drink Josie had poured him; then he just stood there breathing deep and hard. I thought he had drunk that whiskey too fast and it had shot up to his brains. I asked him what was the matter, but he turned away from me. He started toward the front like he was definitely going somewhere; then all of a sudden, like he had just remembered he didn't have any place in the world to go, he stopped, looked quickly each way, then slammed Murphy Bacheron up 'side the head. I supposed he hit Murphy because Murphy was closest to him, but he couldn't have picked a worse choice.

# 22

For about five seconds—it looked more like five minutes—nobody moved. Because nobody thought Murphy had been hit, and that included Murphy. Nobody who knew Murphy was crazy enough to hit him, so it took about five seconds for everybody to realize what had happened. Then it started—Murphy screamed. Not from pain—no, Marcus hadn't hurt him that much; he screamed because all of a sudden he realized he hadn't had a good fight in about a year. So he screamed and hit Black Ned. He didn't hit Marcus—he wanted to save Marcus for later; he hit Black Ned. When Black Ned got up, he hit Jocko Thompson. Jocko didn't go down, and he rammed his fist into one of the Aguillard boys's stomach. One of the other brothers saw what Jocko did and hit Jocko in the back.

Now, I was no more than a couple feet away from that back door when Marcus hit Murphy Bacheron, but by the time Murphy hit Black Ned I was halfway across the kitchen. I wasn't trying to get there, I still don't know how it happened. I've been in house fights and bar fights, and I know the best thing for you to do is get out quick as you can. That probably was in my mind (I'm sure it was), but some kind of way I found myself halfway across the kitchen. I wasn't fighting, mind you, I was just trying to get back to that door.

But like a man trying to swim against a stiff wind, every time I got close, the crowd would knock me back.

"Goddamn you," I heard Josie saying. "Goddamn you, Snuke Johnson."

Josie was cursing Snuke Johnson and trying to push her way toward Marcus at the same time. But there was a crowd of people between her and Marcus, and every time she pushed one foot forward, the crowd pushed her that far back.

"You sonofabitch you, Snuke Johnson," she said, still trying to get to Marcus. "You sonofabitch you."

Then somebody got thrown against the wall, and a bunch of pans and spoons and pots and cups and tops all fell down.

"Who hit me? Now, who hit me?" I heard Sun Brown saying. "Who hit me? I want to know the exact man who hit me. I ain't after hitting nobody but the exact man who hit me. I'm a peace-loving and—"

I heard a hit and a groan.

"Oh Lord, now I'm mad," Sun said. "The same sonofagun done hit me again."

Then somebody else got slammed against the wall and something else fell—probably a tub.

"Oh goddoggit, I'm the maddest man in the house now," I heard Sun Brown saying.

"Snuke Johnson, you sonofabitch," I heard Josie saying. "You sonofabitch you."

All this time I was pulling on people, pushing on people, squeezing through people, trying to get to that back door. Nothing happened to me until I was one step from it, until I could smell the good air, until I had cocked up my leg to jump. Then somebody said, "Don't leave us now, Kelly, the fun just starting." And he or somebody else cracked me over the shoulder with something that felt like a rolling pin. As I started down—I wasn't out—but as I started down I grabbed hold to the first thing I touched. It was soft and fleshy but I didn't care.

"Get your hands off my ass," I heard a woman saying from a long way off. "You horny son—goddamn you, get your hands down."

I wanted to tell the woman I wasn't after feeling her ass. All I wanted was to stay on my feet long enough to reach that door because I was afraid if I went down I was going to be trampled to death. I was screaming these words inside, but they wouldn't come out. They wouldn't even come out in a whisper.

"Get 'em down," she said, hitting me on the hands. "God-damn it, I mean, get 'em down."

I recognized Josie's voice and I tried to explain why I was holding on, but the words still wouldn't come out. And she went right on hitting me. She beat me on one hand for a while, then she twist to the other side and beat me on the other hand. Finally I went down. I didn't move for a couple seconds, then I started crawling toward the door. Before I could get there somebody fell on me and knocked me flat on my face.

"Kelly," Black Ned said, and hit me on the same shoulder that the other person had hit me with the rolling pin. "You wouldn't get me that beer, huh, you no-good sonofabitch."

He hit me in the side and 'cross the head. Before I could hit him back he was already up in the air. It had happened so quick, I didn't see it happening. One second he was on the floor hitting me 'cross the head, the next second he was in the air kicking like a fish on a string. Somebody had him by the collar with one hand, slapping him around with the other.

I tried to crawl toward that back door again, but with so many legs around me I didn't know if I was going toward the door or the window. Then somebody picked up the tub of ice water that the beer had been in and dumped all that on my back.

"Oh Lord," I screamed.

I tried to push myself up, but somebody else fell on me. This one was softer and heavier than Black Ned, so I figured it wasn't him again. It wasn't; it was Josie.

"You sonofabitch you, Snuke Johnson," she said. "You sonofabitch you."

"I'm not Snuke Johnson, Josie," I said.

"You sonofabitch you, Snuke Johnson," she said, looking at me. "You sonofabitch you."

I thought Josie had finally gone crazy. I pushed myself up real slowly, then I reached down and pulled her up.

"You all right, Josie?" I said.

"You sonofabitch you, Snuke Johnson," she said, turning from me. "You sonofabitch you."

"That's the way you fight, Kelly?" one of the Aguillard boys said next to me. He swung but I blocked it and clipped him before his punch got through. He went down on the floor like somebody had grabbed both of his ankles.

Just about then Jocko Thompson threw Black Ned on that hot stove, and Black Ned sprung up in the air almost to the ceiling. While he was coming back down, somebody stuck his fist under Black Ned's chin and Black Ned slammed against the stove again. This time he disconnected the pipe. The pipe fell first, then the stove came down. By then, though, one of the Aguillard brothers had seen what I had done to his other brother and he clipped me 'side the ear and down I went.

"You again, Kelly?" the one on the floor said, and hit me in the chest.

By then, though, that hot stove and those hot coals were

beginning to mix with that ice water on the floor, and no-body in his right mind wanted to be down there. So I got up before the Aguillard boy did, and as he tried to grab my leg, I jerked it back and landed a shoe up 'side his face. He went over groaning, and I turned just in time to catch one of the others swinging on me. I went under his fist and clipped him hard and he went down to join his brother on the floor. Then they started fighting each other. The place was so full of steam and smoke you didn't know who was who now.

Some kind of way I made it to the middle door, and just as I stepped into the front room, Murphy Bacheron nodded and spoke my name like he hadn't seen me in a long time; then he hit me so hard I saw a dozen different color stars. The punch didn't knock me out because I heard Murphy saying, "Honor munks gent'mans."

That's all I remembered of the fight, but the next day Jack Claiborn told me the rest. He said he was fighting one of the Aguillard brothers in the front room when he saw Murphy hit me. He said I fell back in the kitchen and about a minute later I came out (out of that steam and smoke) like a man drunk, but a man ready to do anything to get out of there. He said I staggered through the front room, out on the gallery, then down the steps. He said I bent over and picked up Marcus out of the grass and dew where Murphy had thrown him a few minutes before, and I put Marcus on my shoulder and carried him all the way home. There I dumped him on the gallery, then I went to my room and went to bed.

I don't know if all this is true, but I do know that when I woke up the next morning I was laying on the bed with all my clothes on. When I went outside I saw Marcus laying on the gallery still asleep.

# PART TWO

# 23

Monday, twelve o'clock, Marcus started looking at Bon-bon's wife. He was riding on the tractor with me, and as we went by the house I saw him looking at her on the gallery. I didn't think too much of it then because I thought he was still hooked on Pauline. But Louise had seen him looking at her, and when we came back down the quarter I saw how she had shifted that chair so she could face the road better. Marcus looked at her again but he didn't say anything to me about her. Since I didn't think he was looking at her on purpose, I didn't say anything either.

Marcus was still pretty bruised up from the fight last Saturday night. He had already told me what had happened before Murphy Bacheron knocked him out and threw him outside. He said he had knocked out one guy himself and had thrown him through the window. Then he saw this woman hiding in the corner. As he started toward her the woman started screaming. "Shut up," he told her.

"Oh, please, Mr. Convict, I got two little bitty children," the woman cried. "Please, I got two little bitty children, and I'm all they got."

He said he grabbed her and kissed her very hard. ("That's the best thing for 'em when they carrying on like that at a fight," he said.) While he was making her toes curl from his blazing kisses, he felt somebody touching him on the shoulder. He didn't pay the person any mind, he went on kissing the woman. He said he had ideas of forgetting this fight now and jumping through the window with the woman under his arm. The person touched him on the shoulder again. He still didn't pay him any mind. The person touched him a third time. He said he turned and saw this old, scarred-up man standing in front of him with this old derby setting just on the top of his head. He said he wondered where the old man had come from, because anybody who had been there any length of time not only had lost his hat, he had lost half of his clothes. He said to the old man, "Yeah, what you want, grandpa? Can't you see when a man busy?"

He said the old man said, "It 'pears to me lak you was the young gent'man who started dis li'l commotion." Marcus said he started to tell the old man to go home and get his rest and he would talk about it with him the next day, but just about then the old man turned around, blocked a punch, and knocked out the guy who was trying to hit him in the back. He turned to Marcus again.

"People like Harry got no honor," he said. "And I think there ought to be honor munks gent'mans. What you think?"

Marcus said he knew he had to hit this old man before the old man hit him, so he pretended there was somebody else coming up behind the old man. "Watch it," he said. "Watch out." The old man snapped his head around, Marcus threw up his fist to clip him, but before his fist could get through, the old man was facing him again.

"What?" the old man said, ducking to the side. "And I had just told you 'bout honor." Marcus said that was all he heard, that was all he remembered. The next day when he woke up on the gallery, the left side of his face felt like somebody had hit him with a mallet.

Marcus told me all this Sunday evening when we were sitting out on the gallery. Sunday morning after I had cleaned up, I went down the quarter to help Josie clean up her place. Couple the other fellows were down there, too. When we got through, Josie gave us a pint. We stood in the kitchen drinking and talking about the fight; then I went back to the house. Miss Julie Rand and Marcus were sitting out on the gallery. Miss Julie waved a pasteboard fan slowly before her face.

"Miss Julie," I said.

"How are you, Mr. Kelly?" she said, in that little, high-pitched voice.

Miss Julie was sitting in a chair Marcus had brought out of my room. She wore a purple dress; the dress was silk and it shined like new tin. Miss Julie had probably got it out of her trunk or the armoire, because it had a little of that odor I had smelt in her room that night. The dress was long and pleated and came all the way to her shoes. She wore old, high-topped shoes with wooden heels. The shoes didn't have strings, they had buckles. On the floor 'side her chair was her old pocketbook. The pocketbook was black and shiny with brass knobs. I sat on the gallery against the post. Miss Julie waved the fan before her face a couple times. It was one of those old pasteboard fans that undertakers donate to churches every four or five years. It had a picture of Jesus Christ on one side. On the other side was writing, probably the address of the undertaker parlor.

"Well," Marcus said, "I suppose y'all want talk and don't want me round."

He got up and went inside.

"What happened to his face?" Miss Julie said. "Yours—what happened to yours?"

I touched my bottom lip. It was swole and it still hurt a little. My left shoulder was still hurting me, too.

"Bunch of us got in a fight last night at the fair," I said.

Miss Julie moved the fan slowly before her face and looked down at me.

"Marcus didn't start it, did he?" she said. "He's a good boy."

"No ma'am, he didn't start it," I said.

"Sounds like something one of them Aguillard boys might do," she said.

"I don't know who started it," I said.

"But it wasn't Marcus?"

"No ma'am, I don't think so," I said.

"Thanks, Mr. Kelly," she said. "I'm glad I heard it from you. I'm go'n do little visiting while I'm here, and I'm sure they'll be talking 'bout it."

I sat against the post, looking across the gallery. I could feel Miss Julie looking down at me. I could hear the ruffling of her silk dress when she waved the fan before her face. After a while I raised my head and looked at her. In the daylight she looked even older. Her skin had the color of a ripe prune. It was just as wrinkled as a ripe prune. But her eyes were still quick, sharp, piercing and knowing. And she knew I had lied about Marcus. She knew all the time he had started the fight. But she knew I knew what she wanted to hear. She was sharp, all right; she had picked well when she picked me to look after him. She knew I would do what she wanted me to do, I would say what she wanted to hear.

"How's he getting 'long with Sidney out there?" she said.

"All right," I said.

She moved the fan slowly before her face and looked down

at me with those sharp, knowing eyes—telling me she knew everything wasn't "all right" with Marcus and Sidney Bonbon. She knew Marcus and Sidney Bonbon too well to believe that everything was all right. Yet, she knew I knew what she wanted to hear. And she didn't want to hear the truth.

"Marcus talked to Mr. Marshall?" she asked.

"I don't think so," I said.

"You think I ought to talk to Mr. Marshall again?"

"I don't think you need to, Miss Julie," I said "Marcus will make out all right long as he do his job."

She looked down at me with those sharp old eyes that pierced at the heart.

"I worked for them forty years," she said. "Forty years, Mr. Kelly. I never asked for a' extra penny; never even asked for a' extra piece of bread. Forty years, Mr. Kelly."

I nodded.

"I ain't saying they owe me nothing. Because they was good people to me when I was there. But it's the good people you go to when you in trouble, ain't it?"

"Yes ma'am, I suppose so."

"Yes, it's the good people," she said. "But sometimes even good people forget. They don't try to forget—but sometimes they forget. Sometimes they need reminding what you did."

"I'm sure he won't forget what you did for his family," I said.

She nodded.

"How's he doing out in the field?"

"All right."

"Sidney never threat to hit him or anything?"

"No ma'am," I said.

"And that sack?" she said.

"Sack?" I said.

She didn't answer, she just looked at me with those sharp old eyes that pierced to the heart. I didn't know she knew anything about the sack. But I supposed she had seen the same thing done to somebody else.

"He had to pull it," I said. "But every day he pulls it less and less. He's learning how to keep up now."

"Talk to him, Mr. Kelly," she said.

"I do what I can."

"The Lord will pay you back even if I can't."

I looked down at the floor. It always make me shame-face when old people start telling me what the Lord's going to do for me.

"It's hot, isn't it?" Miss Julie said after a while.

"Burning up," I said.

It was about twelve o'clock, and that sun was so hot you had to half shut your eyes to see anything out there.

"I brought some food there," she said. "A nice cake. I told him half of it was for you."

"Thank you," I said.

"Ehh, Lord, it's hot," she said. Then she looked over her shoulder and called, "Marcus?"

He didn't answer her. She didn't call again, like she knew he had heard, like she knew he would come sooner or later. After a while he showed up.

"You feel all right?" she asked him.

"Sure, nan-nan," he said.

"You need anything?"

"I can use couple bucks if you got it."

She reached over and got the old pocketbook off the floor. After clicking it open, she pulled out an old pocket handkerchief. It took her so long to untie the handkerchief, I started to ask her if she needed help. Marcus just stood there waiting, not even looking at her.

"There," she said, and caught her breath.

She spread the handkerchief out in her lap and picked up several old, rolled-up bills. She unrolled the bills and looked at them a long time. She was wondering how much she could give him. She probably had to save some money for things she needed in Baton Rouge. She reached him a five-dollar bill. He didn't say thanks or anything; he didn't even nod his head.

"Ehh, it's hot," she said, after she had tied up her handkerchief and stuffed it back into the old pocketbook again. "Well, I think I'll go down and see some of the people," she said. "Now, you sure you don't need me to do anything in there?" she asked Marcus.

"What?" I thought. "And you had to rest from untying a pocket handkerchief."

"Everything all right," he said. "I got plenty food. When George picking you up?"

"Sometime this evening," she said. "Ehh, Lord, it's hot. I hate to even stand up."

She got up and just stood there, looking out in the yard. Then she said, "Ehh, Lord," again and started down the steps. I took her by the hand and helped her to the ground. She bowed to me and thanked me and went out of the yard. Marcus was standing in the door; he wasn't even looking at her.

# 24

So now he was looking at Bonbon's wife. I didn't know it then—I mean I didn't know he was doing it with the notion of taking it any farther. I thought he was looking at her just like all of us looked at her when we went by the house. We knew she wanted to give it to us—any of us who was crazy enough to come in there and get it—but we all knew the trouble that could follow.

Marcus went back to the yard with me Monday evening, and when we came back down the quarter, Sidney Bonbon's dog barked at us.

"They got a dog, too, huh?" he said.

"Yeah," I said.

I didn't give it another thought after that. Anybody else who didn't know about the dog would have asked that same question. But Marcus was already wondering how he was going to get by that dog into that house.

But the funny thing about all this, Marcus didn't know Louise had been looking at him for a week already. If he had, I doubt if he would have wanted Louise. Because, you see, he wanted her only for revenge. He wanted to get to her, not her getting to him. He wanted to clown for her, he probably would have stood on his head for her, probably would have walked on his hands for her—until he got into those drawers. Then that would have been the end. If they lynched him after, it wouldn't have meant a thing. Because, you see, they couldn't take away what he had got. No, he probably would have laughed at his lynchers.

Marcus thought about all this Saturday evening while he was unloading those two trailers of corn; because before that time Marcus hadn't given Louise a moment's thought—not one. It was just Pauline. But up there unloading those trailers, things started changing. He saw Pauline again. She came out of the house and went across the yard, and she didn't even glance at him. Yet, she stopped to talk to Bonbon, who met her between the house and the big gate. Marcus, pitching corn into the crib, could see them talking. The longer he watched them, the madder he got. Then she went out of the yard. He could see her slip through the thin dress. He could see how that slip clung to her slender body. He thought how he would be a completely different person with a lovely body like that to come home to. Then he realized that that body was for a white man, and he got mad again. He wanted to hurt her. He wanted to really hurt her. But how? Beat her up? Kill one of her children? Yes, yes, that would hurt her. But what would that do to Bonbon? Probably nothing. What did Bonbon care about two little mulatto children?

Marcus pitched corn and thought. The hot corn dust had his eyes and body on fire.

How could he hurt Bonbon? How? How? Wait; wait. Yes—sure. Bonbon had a wife, too, remember. Yes, that's right, he had a wife. And some kind of way he would get to his wife. So let them lynch him—let them. What did he care.

"No," he thought; "they ain't lynching me. I'm go'n run away from this goddamn place. That's what I'm go'n do—but when? If I try now they'll throw me in Angola for the rest of my life. It won't be for no five years, it'll be for the rest of my natural life. No, I can't run now. I have to wait until that trial over. Then I'll pick my chance . . .

"But suppose they put that trial off for six months? Them white people can do what they want with a nigger. Suppose they put it off for six months? Then what? What then? No. No. Him there laying with her and me laying in that house knowing it—no; hell no. I'd rather die. I'd rather die."

Marcus had unloaded one trailer of corn and was on the second load when Marshall Hebert came from the store and looked up at him. This was the first time he had seen the big white man, but he knew who he was from hearing people talk. Marshall stood there looking up at him a few minutes; then he walked away. Marcus saw him pull a piece of moss from one of the trees, and after rolling it up into a ball, drop it on the ground. He walked across the yard toward the big gate and looked out in the road. But the road didn't interest him, and he turned to look at Marcus. He must have stood by the gate a half hour watching Marcus work.

After Marshall had gone, Marcus started thinking about Bonbon's wife. The thought of taking out his revenge on Louise gave him extra strength to go on. Finally, a little after ten o'clock, he finished up and came down the quarter. And after taking a bath and coming outside, who should he see in the road but Pauline, walking by herself. He said if she had acted toward him the way a woman ought to act toward a man, everything about Bonbon's wife would have been forgotten. But, no, when she saw him she acted like she had seen the devil himself. He said that's why he hit her. He wanted to show her he was a man, not dirt. He said he was so mad with her he wanted to kill her, and, yet, at the same time, if she had given him a little smile, he would have been ready to kill Bonbon for her.

# 25

But now he was looking at Bonbon's wife. He had been looking at her two days before I caught on to what was happening. Monday morning in the field, the two punks made him sweat just like they had made him sweat the week before. When Bonbon came out there in the evening he made him sweat again. But it looked like he didn't mind. I didn't know what had made the change. I didn't know if Bonbon had got the best of him already, or if Murphy Bacheron had done it with that one punch last Saturday night. Tuesday it was the same: the punks in the morning, Bonbon in the evening. Then Wednesday night when we were coming back down the quarter we saw Louise standing near the gate.

Louise was about twenty-five, but she was the size of the average twelve- or thirteen-year-old girl. Most of the time she wore the clothes of a thirteen-year-old girl—she wore skirts and blouses instead of dresses. She wore sandals instead of shoes. She never wore socks or stockings unless it was winter. Her hair was yellow (the same color with that hay in August) and her face was more cream-color than it was white. Her sad gray eyes were the only thing about her that made you feel Louise wasn't a child. They had seen too much sorrow, they had seen it much too long.

I had seen Louise up close only once, when Bonbon sent me from the field to get the gun. Aunt Margaret, the old lady in the quarter who worked for them, wasn't up there that day, so Louise had to bring the gun to the gate. Louise didn't say anything to me, her eyes didn't invite me in; she just stood there with the gun hanging in her hand like she was waiting for me to make the first move. If I wanted to touch her face or her hair, if I wanted to kiss her or push her down, then go right on and do it. She wasn't telling me to do it, but she wasn't telling me not to do it, either. It was left up to me. Burl Colar told me she made him feel the same way once when Bonbon sent him there. But me and Burl both did the same thing; we got away from there quickly as we could. At the same time we were careful to keep people from thinking we were running.

Louise wore a white dress that night when Marcus and I saw her, and under those black, moss-covered trees, she looked like a ghost standing there. At first I thought she was by herself, but as we came closer I saw she was holding Tite by the hand. Tite was her little three-year-old daughter.

"Madame Bonbon," Marcus said, and bowed to her.

She didn't answer. She was looking at him all the time, but she acted like she didn't even hear him. When we got little farther down the quarter, I grabbed him by the arm and jerked him around.

"What you meant back there?" I asked him.

"All I did was speak to her," he said.

"You saw me speaking?"

"I saw you trembling," he said, grinning.

I got mad with him then. I remembered all the other things he had pulled. I remembered that old woman telling me to look after him, to talk to him. I remembered only three days ago she wanted to go to Marshall Hebert again to beg Marshall to keep Bonbon from hurting him or killing him out there in the field. Right now I wanted to hit him so bad my hand started shaking.

"I'm getting sick of you, Marcus, you hear me?"

"All right," he said.

"What you mean by that?"

"You getting sick of me—leave me alone."

We were standing face to face, no more than a foot or two apart. It was dark, but I could see how the sweat and dirt had caked on his face. I wanted to hit him so bad then I wanted to knock his face clean.

"You sonofabitch," I said.

I wanted him to curse me back so I could kick his ass good. He grinned.

"You rotten sonofabitch," I said.

"Now, what you cussing me for?" he said. "All I did was speak to the poor little suffering thing—there you going round cussing me. They ought to have more love in this world."

"You sonofabitch," I said.

He shook his head and grinned. "Going on down the quarter, Jim?" he said.

We started walking again. He walked a little ahead of me. Every now and then he glanced back at me and grinned.

After I ate supper I came out on the gallery with my guitar. Few minutes later Marcus came out there and laid down in front of his door. He was laying on his back looking up at the tin roof. I didn't know if he was listening to me playing the guitar or if he was still thinking about Louise up the quarter.

"Marcus?" I said.

He didn't answer me and I called him again. This time he looked at me and grinned.

"Listen," I said, moving over where he was. I was going to talk to him in a different way now. I wasn't going to get mad again, I was going to talk to him like you talk to a child. "We don't want any trouble on this plantation, hear?" I said.

"What kind of trouble?" he said.

"The kind of trouble Bonbon would make if he caught you messing with his wife. Do you know what he would do if he caught you anywhere near that woman?"

He didn't answer.

"He would lynch you. He would burn you alive. Him and his brothers would burn you alive. You and half of the people around here."

"I just spoke to her," he said.

"Is that all it's going to be?"

He didn't answer.

"Is it?" I said.

"I just spoke to the lady," he said. "I see no harm in speaking to a person."

I could feel myself getting mad again. I didn't want to, I don't like to get mad. But something about Marcus made you mad no matter if you liked it or not.

"Don't fuck with that woman, Marcus," I said. "You hear me?"

He didn't answer.

"You hear me, boy? I don't want to have to kick your ass, now."

"Jim, please," he said. "Just let me digest my food. Can't a man lay down in peace and digest his food after he been working all day."

My hand sprung over his chest. I wanted to grab him, I wanted to shake him, I wanted to slam him against the wall. But my hand just hung over his chest, trembling.

I got up from there and went to my side of the house,

then I threw my guitar on the bed and went down to Josie's. She had some cold beer there and I drank a couple bottles.

"Tell that goddamn convict keep 'way from my place," she said.

"Tell him yourself," I said, "I'm no goddamn messenger."

"What the hell's wrong with you tonight?" she said.

"Nothing," I said. "Here's your money."

I paid her and went out. I stood out in the road a long time, telling myself I ought to get away from here. "I don't owe that old woman anything," I said. "I ought to go pack my bags and get away from here. Sure as hell, that son-ofabitch is going to start trouble before all this is over with."

# 26

Now he was looking for her every time he went by the house; and every time he went by she was looking out for him, too. He had quit riding on the tractor with me; he was riding in the trailer on the corn now. But if I glanced back at him, I would see him watching out for her; if I looked toward the house I would see her sitting out there on the gallery. They would watch each other like that until they couldn't see each other any more for the dust.

But when I said Louise was watching Marcus, I don't mean she made it clear to everybody what she was doing. She never ran to the end of the gallery or smiled or waved or anything like that. What she did was watch him from inside; I mean, she watched him by thinking the same way he was thinking. She knew he had seen her, he was noticing her, so all she had to do now was think the way he thought. No, she never moved, she never smiled, she never waved or anything; she just looked and thought and waited.

Thursday night, Marcus and I were sitting out on the gallery when Bonbon went down the quarter in the truck. We saw the truck stop in front of Pauline's house and we saw the lights go out. A minute or two later, after the dust had settled, Marcus stood up and went out of the yard. I didn't have any idea where he was going—unless he was going up to the church. Sun Brown was the one who told me later what had happened. Sun Brown said he was in front of Joe Walker's old empty house when he heard somebody calling Bonbon's name in front of Bonbon's gate. Sun Brown said it was too dark for him to see who it was, but he could hear the person clear as day. It wasn't too loud, he said, but very, very clear: "Oh, Mr. Bonbon; oh, Mr. Bonbon." Sun said he figured that the person had come from up the quarter, because if he had come from down the quarter he would have seen the truck parked in front of Pauline's house. He said he started walking a little faster to tell the person that Bonbon wasn't at home. But, he said, as he came up to the line fence (that oak tree) he saw Miss Louise coming down the walk toward the gate. And by the time he got to the gate where the person (the convict) was standing, Miss Louise was there, too. Louise had little white-head Tite by the hand. Sun said he heard the convict saying, "Mr. Bonbon home?" He said he could have easily told the convict that Mr. Bonbon was down the quarter at Pauline's, but he figured that Miss Louise would do that much. He said he didn't know if Miss Louise answered the convict or not. All she was doing when he went by was standing there holding Tite by the hand. He said he got all the way to the other line fence (that big pecan tree) and still he couldn't hear if she had answered.

Louise didn't answer Marcus that night, Marcus told me later. She just stood there holding Tite by the hand, looking across the gate at him. He said he didn't know what to make of the look—unless you want to call it dreamy. He said she made him feel like he could have done her anything and she wouldn't have even made a sound. She wore the same white dress she had on the night before. The dress was tight round the waist and it had lace on the sleeves. Marcus said the dress made Louise look like a girl about twelve years old. He said he didn't know before how little her waist was, how scrawny her arms and legs were.

Marcus and Louise looked at each other, then Marcus looked down at the little girl Louise was holding by the hand. He said Tite was just standing there quiet-like, holding on to Louise's hand like she might have been in a little dream all her own. He said he didn't know at the time that she was sick with a bad heart.

He looked at Louise again. She was still watching him in that wandering, dream-like way. He said she reminded him of a person who had been lost in the woods; she had been lost for days and days now and she had seen all kinds of things back there that looked like a human being, but none of them had turned out to be human, and now she was looking at him, wondering if he was.

"I reckond Mr. Bonbon ain't here?" he said.

She still didn't say anything—her face didn't even change. She just stood there looking at him like she was wondering if one of them things in the woods had spoke.

Tite leaned over and slapped at a mosquito on her leg. Marcus said Tite did it so slow, it looked like it took all of her strength just to bend forward.

"Come, Judy," Louise said.

The next day Louise was on the gallery when we went by at twelve. She looked at Marcus when we were going up the quarter, she looked at him when we came back down. That evening he took his bath soon as he got home, and went up to the church. But he must have stayed there only a few minutes (he didn't go inside, he stood outside and looked through the window); then he was going up the quarter again. And again Sun Brown saw him. No, he heard the same low, clear voice: "Oh, Mr. Bonbon; oh, Mr. Bonbon." Sun was coming from up the quarter this time and he said he had just met Bonbon going toward the highway in the truck. So he figured that the person who was calling Bonbon now had come from down the quarter. Sun said as he came closer (he was by that big pecan tree) he saw Miss Louise coming out to the gate. So by the time he got to the gate, Louise and Tite were there, too. Sun said he thought, "Now that's funny; that is funny." He said he never thought that the convict had any idea 'bout getting into Bonbon's yard—what fool would have thought that? He said what he meant by, "That's funny; that is funny," was that the same person was calling at Bonbon's house two nights in a row only minutes after Bonbon had left. He said what made it even more funny was that that same person had been working round Bonbon all day both days. He said what was even funnier still was that this same person should have been the last person in the world to be looking for Bonbon after Bonbon had worked him like he had. But to cap everything, Sun said, was that Miss Louise had come out to the gate twice. He said she had never done that to anyone else long as he had been there, and he had been on the plantation twice as long as she had.

Sun said by the time he got to the gate, Louise was there with little white-head Tite. But this time she was standing much closer. He said he heard the convict say, "Mr. Bonbon home?" He said again he didn't know if she answered him or not. He strained his ears until he got to that other line fence (that big oak tree); then he stopped because he was too far away to hear anything anyhow.

She didn't say anything to him again that night, but Tite did.

"Hello," Tite said.

"Hi," he said. "What's your name?"

"Tite," she said.

"Didn't your mama call you Judy?"

"Judy," Tite said.

"Tite Judy?" he asked.

"Tite," Tite said.

He said he looked down at her. He said he didn't know she was sick then, he just thought she was half crazy.

"Don't Tite mean little?" he said.

"Judy," Tite said.

He said he looked at her and thought she was crazy, then he looked at Louise. Louise was looking at him the same way she had looked at him the night before: she still couldn't make up her mind if he was human or if he was one of them things in the woods.

He was standing close to the gate now and his hand was on the gate post. He said Louise raised her hand very, very slowly to one of the pickets in the gate. Her face had no more changed than if she hadn't even moved. He let her hand stay on the picket a while, then his hand moved there and touched hers. No, it wasn't his hand, he said, it was his finger. He touched her with his finger, and before he knew what was happening, his fingernail was digging into her knuckles. He didn't know why his fingernail did that—he wasn't a tormentor, he was a lover. He wanted to hurt her—yes, yes, he wanted to hurt her, but not with no fingernail. His fingernail did that for half a minute before he knew what was happening. When he caught himself, he drew his finger back. But she didn't move. Her expression hadn't even changed. He said all around them crickets were making noise, frogs were calling for rain, lightning bugs were blinking their little lights. Some kind of bird (he didn't know the name) bust out of the weeds along the ditch, flew by them and across the field. All that time Marcus and Louise were standing there looking at each other across the gate. Then he put the tip of his finger in his mouth and rubbed it lightly over the spot where he had hurt her. He told her with his eyes how sorry he was. He could have spoke the words, he said, because Tite was too busy watching lightning bugs to pay him and Louise any mind. Just when he got ready to lean over and kiss her hand, Louise drew her hand back.

"Come, Judy," she said.

# 27

Saturday, when we came up to the yard, we could see the children standing at the crib. So Marcus and I both knew he wouldn't have to unload corn today, or if he had to he was going to have plenty help. As I drove the tractor up closer, the children all moved back to look at Marcus. Bonbon was there by the time I had turned off the motor and climbed down.

"See you made it," he said.

"Yeah."

He wore a white shirt and brown pants and his white cowboy hat. No khakis today and no boots; brown shoes, shining like new tin.

"Y'all children, there, get on that trailer," he said. "That corn can't unload hisself."

The children climbed up on the trailer and started pitching corn into the crib. But soon they were making a game of it. One would flip up an ear of corn, then the others would throw to hit it before it fell in the crib.

"Hey there," Bonbon said. "What you think this is, a baseball or something? Throw that thing right."

The children quit playing and started working the way he wanted them to do. Bonbon watched them a while to make sure they wouldn't start playing again.

"Mind you up there, now, I don't play, no," he said. "You hear me there, Billy Walker?"

"Yassuh."

"You better."

He turned to me.

"Little bastards," he said.

I glanced up at the children. Children are children, I thought, and soon as you turn your back they'll be playing again.

"Geam, I want you go to New Orleans with me," Bonbon said.

"New Orleans?"

"Yeah. The old man there. Got to pick up a piece for that hay machine."

"Well, I'll have to take a bath and change," I said.

"Yeah, take the truck," he said, nodding toward it over by the tool shop.

"What time you leaving?"

"Soon's you get back. Want get there and come back 'fore night. You need your pay?"

"No, I have a few bucks. I won't be spending anything in New Orleans." I glanced at Marcus and looked at Bonbon again. "I reckond Marcus can attend a little business in Bayonne?" I said.

Marcus didn't have any business to attend in Bayonne (at least he hadn't told me about any), but I thought I would try to get him off any kind of work Bonbon might have had in mind.

"No. Some other time. Today he got to clean up my yard there," Bonbon said.

"Your yard?" I said, almost screaming it out.

Bonbon looked at me surprised. I had never answered him quite so impolitely before.

"Something the matter, Geam?" he said, squinting down at me.

I couldn't answer him. All I could do was frown and shake my head.

"I know what you thinking," Bonbon said. "Them leafs been there ten years and all a sudden she want them raked up. Women—how you figure them, hanh?"

My heart was jumping too much for me to say anything; and I wouldn't dare look at Marcus, either.

I didn't know then that Marcus had seen Louise those two nights, because I hadn't talked to Sun Brown, yet. But I knew he had been noticing her from the tractor and he was just waiting for the chance to get near that house. Once he got there (where both him and her wanted him to get) he was going to make his move.

"So that's your job this evening," Bonbon said. "And mind you, I want that raked, yeah."

"I'll rake it," Marcus said. "Give it the best raking it ever had."

Bonbon was looking at him. Bonbon was three or four inches taller than Marcus, so now he squinted down at him.

No, this didn't have anything to do with Marcus hitting Pauline. Bonbon didn't know what had happened between Marcus and Pauline. Pauline had probably told him she had hit her jaw against a doorknob or that a can of something had fell off the shelf and hit her. Or maybe the clothesline prop had slipped away from the line and hit her while she was hanging clothes. No, this had nothing to do with her. This was all Louise's doing. She had found out that he had to go to New Orleans and he would be gone for at least half a day.

How? How? How? she had probably thought. How? How? How? And probably, while walking across the yard, she had looked down and seen the leaves—leaves that had been laying there ten, maybe twenty years; leaves on top of leaves on top of leaves; leaves that weren't leaves any more, but had turned back to dust. Even if Marcus used a shovel and even if he dug six feet in the ground he would never reach the bottom of all those leaves.

I looked at him now. He knew I was going to look at him, and he knew I was going to look at him then. He wanted to grin. He was grinning inside, he was laughing his head off inside.

"Well, it's going to be cool under those trees," I said. "Nice and cool under there. Almost like a picnic."

"It won't be no picnic," Bonbon said.

"Almost one," I said, still looking at Marcus. "I wouldn't mind having a job like that myself." I turned to Bonbon now. "Couldn't give me that job and take him with you, could you?"

"The old man want you to go."

"Sure," I thought. "The Old Man want me to go. He want him in there. He want Bonbon to find him and her in that bed. Sure, He want that. He want a fire. He want Bonbon to burn the place down. Didn't the Bible say He was going to destroy the world next time by fire? Sure, He want me to go."

"Well, I was figuring that since he's the convict and I'm not I would get the easiest job," I said.

"You get it next time, Geam," Bonbon said.

Marcus coughed; he wanted to laugh. He was laughing so much inside, he was ready to fall against that trailer. And up on the trailer the children had started playing again.

"Hey, what I say up there," Bonbon said.

The children quit playing.

"You better take off, Geam," Bonbon said to me. "You

better go on home and eat," he said to Marcus. "Be at that house one o'clock. That rake and broom waiting there."

"Yes sir," Marcus said. "I'll surely be there, sir. And I'll do a good job, sir. You won't even recognize it when you get back."

When we got in the truck, I turned to him.

"Don't mess with that woman, Marcus," I said.

He grinned. "I'm going there to rake leaves," he said.

"You hear me, don't you?" I said.

"The man want me to rake his leaves," he said. "You don't want me to rake his leaves?"

"I'm warning you," I said.

I started up the truck and drove out of the yard.

# 28

We ate at the same time. I sat at the table, he sat on the steps. I was looking at the back of his curly head. I started to hit him—no, kick him—but what was the use? Do you think kicking him would have done any good? Bonbon had made him pull a sack two weeks and that hadn't done any good; do you think kicking him would have done any good? Murphy Bacheron had almost knocked his head off and that hadn't done any good. I had talked and the old lady from Baton Rouge had talked to him and that hadn't done any good—do you think kicking Marcus would have done any good?

I thought about killing him—shooting him in the head with my gun or hitting him in the head with the axe—but why should I? Why should I go to the pen for something like that? Let him get in that bed with her. He wanted to get there, she wanted him there, so why should I worry?

After I finished eating, I took a bath in that big number three tub. All the time I was sitting in the tub I was thinking about Aunt Margaret. All of my big talk about not caring what Marcus did didn't mean a thing. I would do almost anything in the world to keep Marcus from messing around with Louise. So I thought about Aunt Margaret. I knew it was kind of indecent of me to think about an old Christian lady like that while I was in the bathtub, but I would try almost anything. "Yes, yes," I thought. "Yes, yes, that's it."

By the time I had put my clothes on it was one o'clock. I shut up the doors and windows and went out on the gallery. Marcus was laying there on his back with his legs crossed.

"All right, let's make it," I said.

"You the boss," he said.

After turning the truck around I drove up to Aunt Margaret's house. I didn't see her, but I saw Unc Octave and Mr. Roberts sitting out on the gallery. They were talking about the war when I came into the yard. They talked about the war every time they got together, and that was every day God send. The war had been over three years already, but they talked about it like everybody was still shooting at everybody else. Mr. Roberts had his little switch as usual. He carried it everywhere he went. He used it for popping at flies when they lit on the floor near him. He was pretty good, too. He very seldom missed.

"How y'all feel?" I said.

"So-so, and yourself, Jimmy?" Unc Octave said.

"Pretty hot," I said. "Unc Octave, can I speak to Aunt Margaret?"

"She still up the quarter," he said.

"She's working this evening?"

"She better be working," Unc Octave said.

He and Mr. Roberts both laughed.

"Well, I'll see her up there," I said. "How you feel, Mr. Roberts?"

"Fine, and you, James?"

"Fine," I said. "Well, I'll be seeing y'all later."

They told me good day, and I went back to the truck and drove slowly up the quarter. When I stopped in front of

Bonbon's house to let Marcus out, I got out, too. Just before he went in the yard, I stopped him. I could see the rake and the broom leaning against the fence.

"That's what you work with," I said. "If you want any water there's a hydrant round the back. You hear me, don't you?"

He grinned. He hadn't heard a thing. I knew before telling him he wasn't going to listen; I just thought it was my duty to say it, anyhow.

"You can start working," I said.

"You the boss," he said, and went to the rake.

I looked toward the house and called Aunt Margaret. She didn't show up at first and I called her again. She came out on the gallery. Tite was with her.

"Mind stepping to the gate a minute?" I said.

Aunt Margaret came down the steps holding Tite by the hand. Aunt Margaret was short and fat. Her face was round and black and oily. Her short nappy hair (you could even see her skull) was just starting to turn gray.

Aunt Margaret was funny even when she was sad. If she was fussing at Unc Octave or singing in church, there was something funny by the way she did it. I'm sure even if Aunt Margaret was dying she would do something you didn't expect. She would probably move one of her toes or her eyes would pop open just when you thought they were closed for the last time. Aunt Margaret and I had been friends ever since I came to the plantation. Many times I had ate at her house when I didn't have anything at my house to eat or when I didn't feel like cooking.

"How you feel, Aunt Margaret?" I said, when she came up to the gate.

"All right; yourself?"

"Okay," I said.

Aunt Margaret was pretty strong for somebody her age and she still had a good, strong voice. She was looking at me now like she knew what I had in mind.

"She want her leaves raked, huh?"

Aunt Margaret nodded.

"Been there twenty years, but now all of a sudden she want them raked, huh?"

Aunt Margaret grunted this time, still looking straight in my eyes like she knew what I had in mind.

"Listen, Aunt Margaret," I said.

"Don't have to say it," she said. "I know."

"No, I better say it," I said. "Don't let him get ten feet of that house."

"That dog there."

"That's right, the dog; I forgot about him. Don't let her serve him any water."

"They got a hydrant there."

"She might want to give him some cold water though, or some lemonade."

"He drink hot hydrant water or he don't drink no water," Aunt Margaret said, looking at Marcus and looking at me again. "I hate that trash already. Here good people trying to live in peace and he show up with his mess. What Mr. Marshall brought him here for in the first place? You can't tell me he like Miss Julie Rand that much."

"I suppose he does," I said. "She gave that family forty years of her life."

"Ehh, Lord," Aunt Margaret said. "And I had planned to do me little fishing this evening. But that's over with, though. I won't leave this house 'fore that trashy thing leave even if this world was coming to a' end."

"If you do, it might just do that," I said. "It's in your hand, Aunt Margaret."

"My hand," she said, looking at the hand that wasn't holding Tite. "My hand. All they done done all they life was housework and clean baby mess—'cepting little fishing now and then; now I'm old, they got to protect the world." She looked at Marcus. "Black trash," she said quietly. She looked at me. "Sometimes I think the Master must be 'sleep."

"I think He's tired."

"He must be something."

"What's she doing in there?"

"Laying 'cross that bed resting."

"For this evening, huh?"

"Not if I can help it," Aunt Margaret said. She looked at Marcus raking leaves against the fence. "Not if I can help it, you dirty thing."

"Well, I got to take off," I said. "I'm going to New Orleans with Bonbon."

"New Orleans, my foot," Aunt Margaret said. "He taking her to Baton Rouge to shop."

"What did you say, Aunt Margaret?"

"Just what I said," she said. "He taking Pauline to Baton Rouge to shop."

"He told me—"

"Uh-huh," Aunt Margaret said, cutting me off.

"Louise know about it?"

"Don't she know everything he do?"

"And that's why she want her leaves raked today, huh?"

Aunt Margaret didn't answer me; she looked at Marcus. Both of us looked at him a second, then I told her I was leaving.

# 29

I drove out to the store where I figured Bonbon was wait-
ing for me. He came out and told me to move over, and he
got under the steering wheel. We hadn't gone a quarter of
a mile before I saw Pauline walking 'side the road. She was
in pink and she had on her big white straw hat. Bonbon
stopped the truck and I got out so Pauline could sit in the
middle.

"How's it going?" I asked, when we started moving again.

"Burning up," she said.

She glanced at Bonbon but neither one of them said any-
thing. She even sat a little closer to me than she did to him.

So that's why he needed me, that's why he wanted me to
go with them. Not that a white man couldn't ride all over
the South with a black woman, but if they were traveling
in daytime by themselves, the black woman had to look like
she was either going to work or coming from work. It
wouldn't be safe for her to be dressed like Pauline was now
or to have that powder smelling on her breast like Pauline
did now. No, they wouldn't say anything to Bonbon; they
probably wouldn't say anything to Pauline in front of Bon-
bon. But if they caught her by herself they would definitely
remind her to never do it again. And sometimes they re-
minded you in ways you could never forget.

So that's why they needed me. She was my wife, not his woman. And nobody was going to ask any questions. Even if they knew better they wouldn't ask any questions now.

Bonbon drove about seventy all the way into Baton Rouge. The only time he slowed up was when he came up behind another car. Then soon as he saw daylight he shot around the car and hit seventy again. He and Pauline didn't exchange two words. Pauline glanced at him every now and then when she thought he was going too fast. Once when Bonbon cursed a man for driving too slow, Pauline looked at Bonbon and went, "My, my." Then she looked at me and smiled. She smiled the way a wife smiles after telling-off her husband.

When we came into Baton Rouge, Bonbon went by the hardware store and bought a little piece of iron so little that Tite could have come and gotten it by herself. Then he parked the truck in a parking lot while I went shopping with Pauline. I'm not one of these people who like to shop—I even hate to buy a loaf of bread—but I liked walking around with Pauline. I liked watching her walk in front of me down the store aisles. I liked seeing her pick up things and lay them back down carefully and neatly when she didn't care for them. She had that quality, that real woman quality, that made you like being with her.

"How do you like this?" she asked me. She was holding up a white scarf with polka dots.

"It's beautiful," the white salesgirl said.

Pauline smiled at her respectfully, but she still looked at me. She wanted me to tell her how I thought Sidney Bonbon was going to like the scarf.

"Nice," I said.

When we came to the stockings, she said, "Like these?"

I looked at the stockings and looked down at her legs.

"Yep. Very much," I said.

Pauline smiled at me. The little white salesgirl glanced down at Pauline's legs and didn't raise her head for a while. When you looked at Pauline's legs and looked at her legs you could see why she wasn't in a hurry to look up. Pauline bought a belt for Bonbon, then we left. When we got back to the truck, Bonbon was asleep. His white cowboy hat was pulled over his face.

"Hi," Pauline said.

Bonbon pushed the cowboy hat back and looked at us.

"Make it back, huh?" he said, sitting up.

We got into the truck. Pauline gave Bonbon the little white box with the belt. He opened the box and looked at the belt, then he reached over to put it in the dash drawer.

"Ain't you putting it on?" Pauline said. She was acting just like a wife again.

He didn't answer her. I saw the forty-five in the dash drawer when the door popped open. Bonbon put the belt in there and slammed the door back.

"Where we go?" he said.

"Home," Pauline said, like she was mad.

Bonbon looked at me. "Geam?"

"I'm with y'all," I said.

"Y'all didn't talk?"

I waited for Pauline to answer.

"We talked," she said, looking at him like she was mad. "I asked Jim how he liked my stockings, how he liked my scarf. I bought some things for the children and I asked him how he liked that. I asked him how he liked your belt. He said he liked all of them."

Bonbon squinted down at Pauline from under that cowboy hat. You could tell that Pauline wasn't giving him the answers he wanted to hear. Pauline started looking out at the other cars on the parking lot. Bonbon just kept on looking down at her. I sat against the door, waiting. I hoped they wouldn't start anything. That was something I didn't want to be around.

"Geam, you know a good place we can drink?" Bonbon asked me.

"I think so."

Bonbon paid the parking lot attendant and drove out on the street. We found a bar where a lot of mulattoes hung out. The bar was cool and dark. We sat at a table against the wall and I ordered a set-up. The set-up was a pint of whiskey, a bowl of ice, and a pitcher of water. The waitress brought it over. She was one of those pretty Creole gals with a lot of that jet black hair hanging over her shoulders. When I paid her I looked up at her cream-color face, and she smiled back at me. I told her to keep the change. She nodded and left.

"Lover-boy," Pauline said.

"She's pretty," I said.

I opened the pint of whiskey and set it on the table. Bonbon didn't look like he was going to fix a drink for him or Pauline, so I asked Pauline if she wanted me to fix her one. She said yes, and I fixed it and handed it to her. She nodded and said it was just right.

"Fix you one?" I asked Bonbon.

"Yeah," he said.

I fixed it and Pauline handed it to him. He didn't say thanks or anything. He drank and set the glass on the table. His white cowboy hat was on the table, too.

I fixed a drink for myself and took a good swallow.

"Ah, this is the life," I said.

I thought this would get a conversation going, but nothing happened. All three of us just sat there looking at the other people in the place. You had some black skin in there, but most of them were mulattoes. I supposed they took Bonbon for a mulatto, too. He was darker than many of them.

We finished one drink and started another one. Pauline tried to start a conversation with Bonbon, but he just sat there looking at the other people. I remembered he had brought the gun out of the truck with him. You could see the print of it stuck under his shirt. He needed it everywhere he went. He needed it around his own Cajuns, he needed it around the Negroes in the field, and even needed it around these mulattoes who didn't know him at all. He was a man who needed a gun no matter where he was.

"Hi," Pauline said softly to him.

Bonbon didn't look at her. He was still looking at the other people in the place.

"Hi," she said, softly again.

He looked at her from the side. She put her small hand on his big hand that was holding the glass. Then she started rubbing her finger over his wrist. She said something to him very softly and he leaned over to hear what she had said. She made him lean even closer to her so she could whisper in his ear. She put her hand on his shoulder and whispered in his ear a long time. Then he picked up his glass and drank. She kept on looking at him. She looked at him so long he had to look back at her again. He didn't look straight at her, he looked at her from the side. But even from that side glance you could see how much he cared for her. For a second there they looked at each other like they were the only two people in the place. Just him and her in this cool, dark place, all by themselves.

I moved my chair back and that broke the spell. That reminded him of everything. That reminded him that he was white and she was black. That reminded him of the mulattoes in the place. That reminded him of the white people outside who didn't go for this kind of mixing in public.

"Where you going, Geam?" he said.

"Down the block a piece. I know a gal down there."

"You got a gal here. The one give us that whiskey."

"No, I'm going down the block," I said, walking off.

"Geam?" he said. Two long strides and he was 'side me. "Geam, this a good place?"

"You don't have to worry."

"I mean for us?"

"It's a good place," I said. I nodded toward the bar. "Talk to that fat man at the other end of the bar. He'll fix you up."

"You talk to him."

I shook my head. "No sir."

He looked at me hard. He didn't like it when I said I wasn't going to be his pimp. He glanced over his shoulder at Vincent deLong who owned the place, then he looked at me again. He didn't know how to go to a man like Vincent deLong, that's why he wanted me to do it. That's why he had wanted Pauline to talk to me before. He was helpless in a case like this. He wanted to be with her—yes, you could tell from watching them at the table how much he loved her and wanted to be with her; but he had to go to a black man, in a respectful way, and ask that black man for a room. He didn't know how to do that. He didn't know how to talk to a black man unless he was giving orders.

"I'll see you," I said, and went out.

# 30

I didn't have a girl down the block, but I wasn't going to sit at that table and watch them play with each other. I wasn't going to be his pimp—and I wasn't going to sit in that bar while they laid together in one of deLong's rooms, either.

I went to another bar a couple blocks away and got myself a beer. I sat at a table by myself. There were other people in the place, laughing and talking—some of them dancing—but I didn't pay them any mind. I was thinking about Bonbon and Pauline, and I was thinking about Marcus and Louise. And I thought to myself it was the Old Man. He created them. He didn't create the situation because He knew all the time they would do that themselves. He created them and created me and said, "All right, that'll be your hell. Look after them."

"Why me?" I probably said. "Why me? I like doing just what they like doing. Why do I have to give it up and—"

"Shut up," He probably said.

But maybe it didn't happen like that at all. Maybe He didn't care how it went. He had stopped caring long ago. He didn't even shake his head any more when He saw them doing something they didn't have any business doing. Just like He didn't shake His head when He made a bad move playing chess (by Himself); or when He overlooked a play in solitaire. He just took it like it was part of the game.

No, it wasn't the Old Man. I had put my own self in this predicament. I had come to this plantation myself, when my woman left me for another man in New Orleans and when I was too shame-face to go back home. I had heard that Hebert needed a man who could handle tractors and I had come here for the job. No, it wasn't the Old Man, it was me. It was me when I showed Bonbon I was good with any machine he had there. Maybe if I hadn't showed him how good I was he wouldn't have put so much trust in me. He wouldn't have treated me different from the way he treated all the others. He wouldn't have told me things about himself, things about his family—things he never told anybody else. No, I had to show him how good I could handle tractors. And every time I did, he told me a little bit more. But I'm not saying he told me everything. I'm not saying he put all his trust in me—because I don't think he trusted himself that much. What I'm saying is that he looked to me as somebody he could talk to. He needed to talk to somebody. By the time I came there he had cut himself off from everybody there except Pauline. He went hunting and fishing with his brothers, but he had little to do with the rest of the people. And the reason was Pauline. The others didn't mind if he had this black woman. Everybody expected the white overseer to have a black woman—even his wife expected that. But when he started neglecting his wife for this black woman, then that was a different thing. The whites didn't like that at all, and the Negroes giggled about it. Bonbon knew how both sides felt, and he knew he couldn't go to either of them. So when I, a stranger, came along—somebody who knew all about tractors and trucks—he was glad to have somebody to talk to. At first he talked only about the machines on the

147

plantation. But as we got to know each other, he told me about other things. He told me about his fishing and hunting. He told me about fights among the Cajuns on the river. He told me about how poor he was as a child. He told me he had never gotten any more than a third-grade education. He never talked to me about Pauline or Louise, but he told me about Louise's people that he hated. And every so often he would say something about Pauline's two little boys that he was very proud of. I'm not saying that Bonbon went rattling off at the mouth about all these things. What I'm saying is that Bonbon needed somebody to talk to just like anybody else needs somebody to talk to. And since I knew all about trucks and tractors, I was the person he chose.

I finished one beer and ordered another one. Then I sat back at my table again. No, it wasn't the Old Man. Just like it wasn't the Old Man who had stuck Marcus on me. If I had told Bonbon that night I was too busy to go to Baton Rouge, I wouldn't have met Miss Julie Rand. But, no, I had to go. And once I got there and saw what she was doing to me, I didn't have the nerve to turn her down. Knew what Marcus was, knew he would stick a Texas jack in me just as soon as speak to me, and still I let myself be fooled into taking the job.

No, it wasn't the Old Man. The Old Man didn't have a thing in the world to do with it. It was me—it was my face. Anybody who sees this face feels like he ought to just use it.

After I finished my second beer, I went back to deLong's place. The truck was still there, but when I went inside I didn't see Bonbon or Pauline. I asked the waitress about them. She nodded to deLong at the end of the bar. I asked him.

"In the house there," he said. "Your friend?"

"My overseer. Plantation across the river."

"I see," deLong said. "Yeah, he asked me that room, I give it to him. I see he bring his gun."

"Yeah, he keeps a gun," I said.

"Poor sonofabitch," deLong said. "Bad, a man need a gun all the time—no?"

"It's bad," I said.

DeLong shook his head.

"How long they got the room for?" I asked him.

"Couple hours."

"How long they been in there?"

"Little more than one hour."

"I'll be back."

I didn't go back to the same bar. I went to a smaller one round the corner and a block up. I had a beer there and came on back. DeLong said he had checked the room and Bonbon was sleeping.

"The woman say they stay another hour," deLong said.

I went back to the second bar and came back an hour later. DeLong was just coming in the bar from making his rounds. He had this big white house to the left of the bar and he rented rooms for just this reason. He didn't have girls in there, that was against the law, but you could bring your own girl and get the room. On Mondays and Fridays you could see all the sheets hanging out on the line in the back yard.

"Woke now, but he stay another hour," deLong said. "Crazy 'bout that black woman—no?"

"Yes," I said.

DeLong laughed. He had a mouth full of gold teeth. I had a beer at the bar just so I could look at the waitress again. Then I went outside and sat in the truck.

# 31

After I drove away, Aunt Margaret went back to the gallery and sat in her rocking chair. She said Tite sat in her lap a while, then Tite wanted to go out in the yard where Marcus was working. She didn't want Tite out there, but Tite started wiggling so much in her lap, she had to let her go.

"Don't come back here crying you sting your leg on a nettle, you hear me?" she said to Tite.

Tite didn't answer. Aunt Margaret watched her go across the yard where Marcus was working. Marcus stopped a moment to say something to her, then he started working again. Tite started jumping.

"That child go'n work herself up there and make her heart pump too fast," Aunt Margaret thought. "Tite?" she called. "Petite?"

Tite jumped again.

"What's wrong with that child out there?" Aunt Margaret called to Marcus.

"Nothing," he said.

He got the broom from against the fence and gave it to her. But the broom was so heavy, Tite could hardly move it.

"You see that boy trying to work that child and hurt her," Aunt Margaret said to herself. "Come here, Tite," she called.

Tite didn't answer.

"Tite?" she called.

"Non," Tite said over her shoulder. "Non, non, non."

"Like mama, like daughter, huh?" Aunt Margaret thought.

"You don't know what it is right now, but give you ten, 'leven more years, you'll be wanting the same thing. . . . Ehh, Lord, look where my mind at," she thought. "I ought to do some ironing while I'm up here, save me from doing it next week. But that stension cord won't reach the gallery, and I got to keep my eyes on that boy."

Aunt Margaret said she sat there, looking at him and Tite raking the leaves. Tite was having trouble moving the big push-broom, and she started jumping again. Marcus went to the tree to break off a limb.

"Convict, what you think you doing?" Aunt Margaret jumped out of her chair and hollered at Marcus.

"Getting her a little broom," he said.

He gave it to Tite and Tite started sweeping with that. Aunt Margaret stood at the end of the gallery watching them a while, then she moved back to her chair by the door.

"My heart go'n be worser than this child heart 'fore this day is over," she said to herself.

Aunt Margaret had been sitting out there about an hour when Louise came out of the bedroom and went back in the kitchen. After getting a drink of water out of the icebox, Louise went out on the back gallery and laid down on the cot. Aunt Margaret could see just her feet, her toes sticking up.

"You can lay down anywhere you want, on anything you want; long as you lay down in the back and he rake them leaves in the front," Aunt Margaret thought.

Now, she was watching both of them—Louise's bare feet one second and Marcus raking the leaves the next second. Tite was working right beside Marcus. Every time he pushed out the rake and drew it in, Tite pushed out her little branch and drew it back. Her white hair looked like a white piece of rag stuck up on a stick.

Aunt Margaret said she thought about her ironing again.

She knew the extension cord couldn't reach the gallery, but if she ironed in the living room, she could always see Louise laying down on the cot. And she figured that watching one or the other was just as good as watching both of them. She had just stood up to go inside when she saw Marshall Hebert's car coming down the quarter. Marshall slowed up long enough to look at the boy through the fence, then he went on. Aunt Margaret went to the back gallery to get the ironing board. She had to lean over Louise and the cot to get the ironing board out of the corner. Louise was laying there, looking through a magazine. She didn't look up once. She flipped through the magazine like she had gone through it a thousand times, like she knew all the time what was on the next page even before she got there. Aunt Margaret said after she had pulled the board from among all the shovels and hoes and rakes and axes, she looked down at Louise again. Louise wore a thin green blouse and a white pleated skirt. Instead of buttoning the blouse all the way down, she had tied the two ends in a knot, leaving part of her belly showing. Her white skirt, that didn't go much farther than her knees when she was standing up, was way up her thighs now. Aunt Margaret looked down at her painted toenails and looked back at the magazine. She wanted to look at Louise's face, but Louise wouldn't lower the magazine far enough.

Aunt Margaret went back in the living room with the ironing board. She got the iron off the mantelpiece and connected it to the light socket that hung down from the ceiling. While the iron was getting hot, she went out on the gallery to check on Marcus. Marcus and Tite were coming toward the house.

"Just where you think you going?" Aunt Margaret asked him.

"Water," he said.

"Hydrant in that back yard," Aunt Margaret said.

"Tite told me where it was."

Marcus's face and shirt were wet with sweat. Two lines of sweat ran down the sides of Tite's face, too.

As Marcus and Tite went around the house, the dog came from under the house and started barking at Marcus. He followed them all the way to the back, growling at Marcus through the fence.

Aunt Margaret looked through the house now, and she could see that Louise's toes were pointed the other way. "You see that wench trying to show that boy something he ain't—" Aunt Margaret said, and started toward the back. When she got back there, Marcus had turned on the hydrant and was letting the water run in the barrel.

"Drink and get on back to the front," Aunt Margaret said.

"That water hot," Marcus said.

"It ain't that hot," Aunt Margaret said. "Drink and get on back to them leaves."

"I ain't scawling myself with that hot water," he said. "Y'all got anything cold in there—lemonade or anything?"

Aunt Margaret said she didn't say anything, she just looked at him. She said she didn't want cuss with the next day being her 'Termination Sunday.

She said all the time Marcus was letting the water run in the barrel, he was looking at Louise laying there on the cot. But Louise pretended he wasn't anywhere around. Laying there with half of her belly out and with that skirt pulled halfway up her thighs, and still pretending he wasn't anywhere around. Aunt Margaret said she tried to block out much of Louise as she could, but no matter how she stood, Marcus was still able to see some part of Louise's body. And from the way Louise was laying down there, looking at her painted toenails could cause as much trouble as looking at her belly.

"Didn't I tell you to drink and get back to the front?" Aunt Margaret said.

"All right, I reckond it's cool enough," he said.

He lowered his head and drank from the hydrant. When he raised up again, Tite asked him to let her drink.

"No, you don't," Aunt Margaret said. "She got a cup in here and she got ice water to go in it."

"Can't have none, Tite," he said.

"Dolo," Tite said, jumping. "Dolo, dolo."

"That old lady standing on that gallery say you can't have none," he said.

"Dolo," Tite said, jumping. "Dolo, dolo."

He picked her up and held her to the hydrant.

"Now, duck your head to the side," he said. "Don't stick your tongue out like a snake, duck your head to the side. To the side, Tite."

He put her down. She started jumping again.

"Shut up," he said, "you go'n have some. Now look at me. See what I do." He drank. "See?"

"Wee," Tite said.

He picked her up.

"All right now, duck your head to the side. To the side, to the side, Tite."

Aunt Margaret said she stood there looking at that convict trying to drown that child, and that woman, the child's own mon, just laying there with that skirt pulled halfway up her thighs, not saying a word. She said the dog said more—at least he was still growling at the convict through the fence.

Marcus put Tite down again.

"Now, get back to the front," Aunt Margaret said.

"Got to turn the water off," he said.

"Turn it off and get back to them leaves."

All the time he was twisting the knob on the hydrant, he was looking at Louise laying down on the cot. Then Aunt

Margaret saw him grin. She turned quickly to look at Louise. Louise raised the magazine up to her face again. Aunt Margaret turned to Marcus.

"I told you to get moving," she said. "I mean just that."

"Come on, Tite," he said.

Tite took his hand and they went around the house. The dog followed them, barking at Marcus through the fence. Aunt Margaret said Louise was holding the magazine up to her face like she was reading. But Aunt Margaret knew she wasn't reading, because she could hardly read or write her own name.

Aunt Margaret went back to the front gallery. She could see Tite and Marcus going across the yard holding hands. Marcus picked up his rake and Tite picked up her branch and they went back to work.

Aunt Margaret stood there another five minutes watching them. Marshall Hebert's car went back up the quarter. As he went by the yard, he slowed up and looked at Marcus through the fence again.

Aunt Margaret moved back inside and started ironing. She had finished two of Bonbon's white shirts when Louise got up and came out to the front gallery. Louise stood in the door and looked across the yard where Marcus and Tite were working. Standing there barefooted, she looked more like a twelve-year-old child than she did a twenty-five-year-old woman, Aunt Margaret said.

"Judy?" Louise called.

"Wee, Mama?" Tite answered.

"Don't work too hard," Louise said.

Aunt Margaret stopped ironing and looked at Louise standing in the door, because she knew it wasn't Judy, Louise was talking to, it was Marcus. Louise turned from the door and went back to her room. Aunt Margaret started ironing again.

# 32

Aunt Margaret thought about church the next day and started singing. She thought about the people who were going to be there, how they were going to be dressed and where they were going to be sitting. She knew that Aunt Polly Williams liked sitting by that first window near the pulpit. Aunt Polly would come to church before any of the other members just to get that seat. If anybody else sat there before she did, she would be mad all day. Sometimes Glo Hawkins did that just to make Aunt Polly mad. Once they had a fight in the church. Aunt Polly told Glo Hawkins to move, and Glo Hawkins told her to go sit down. Aunt Polly started beating Glo Hawkins over the head with her pocketbook, and it took three or four other people in church to stop her. Aunt Margaret, thinking about Aunt Polly, had to smile to herself. She thought about the other people who wouldn't be able to come to church because of sickness. Whenever she thought about the sick people, it always made her sad.

Aunt Margaret heard noises in Louise's bedroom. It sounded like Louise was pushing something heavy across the floor. Aunt Margaret stopped singing and listened a moment. Louise stopped pushing whatever it was she was moving. Aunt Margaret thought it sounded like the dresser. She started singing again. Louise started moving the dresser again. Aunt Margaret laid her iron on the side and went out on the gallery. But Marcus was raking leaves just like he was supposed to be doing. Aunt Margaret came back inside and started ironing and singing, and the moving started all over again. Aunt Margaret stopped and listened; the moving stopped. She started singing; the moving started. She stopped and faced the door. She was still humming her church song to herself, but she was humming so low she was sure Louise couldn't hear it. All the time she faced the door, she couldn't hear a sound.

Aunt Margaret went quickly to the front door, and this time she saw Marcus looking toward the house. She moved toward the end of the gallery just as fast as she had come outside, and looked around the corner of the house at Louise's bedroom window, but she saw nothing but the curtains. She thought if she stood there long enough she would see the curtains move, but they never did. Aunt Margaret moved away from the end of the gallery and looked at Marcus again. He had gone back to work; Tite was working right beside him.

Aunt Margaret went back inside and started ironing. Everything was quiet in Louise's room now. Even when Aunt Margaret started singing again, nothing happened in the room.

Fifteen minutes after she had been inside, she saw Marcus and Tite coming toward the house. They went around the house to the hydrant, and a minute later Aunt Margaret heard the water running in the barrel. She stepped back from the ironing board to look at Marcus drinking; then he was holding Tite up so she could drink.

" 'Nough?" he asked Tite.

"Wee," Tite said.

Marcus and Tite started for the front, and Aunt Margaret moved back to her ironing board. She hadn't been ironing a minute, she said, when she heard a loud, booming noise in Louise's bedroom. She jumped around and faced the door, then she went to the door and asked Louise what was the matter. Louise didn't answer. Aunt Margaret heard another noise; it sounded like two people moving fast and trying to be quiet at the same time.

"Wait," Aunt Margaret said. "I know this ain't what I think it is."

She ran to the front door and looked across the yard, but she didn't see Marcus or Tite. She ran back through the house to the back gallery, but she didn't see them by the hydrant, either. Now, she ran back to the front, and this time to the end of the gallery, to look around the side of the house. Tite was standing outside the fence, letting the dog lick her hand. Marcus was nowhere in sight.

Aunt Margaret started to holler at Tite, but she remembered Tite's bad heart. She was scared, too, if she hollered and Tite jerked her hand back too quickly, the dog might bite her. So she broke away from the end of the gallery and ran toward the steps, but after going halfway down, she ran back up again.

"Master," she said. "Master."

She broke inside and started beating on the door with her fist.

"Come out of there, boy," she said, beating. "I mean, come out of there, come out of there."

She heard something slam against the wall—it sounded like a piece of furniture.

"What was that?" she called. "What hit there?"

Nobody answered. Then she heard the same noise again.

It might have been a chair one of them was throwing against the wall.

Aunt Margaret moved back to hit the door with her shoulders. She said she knew that that little frail latch would fly off even if Tite had hit that door hard enough. She hit it. But like she had hit one of those oak trees out in the yard, she went falling back on the floor. "What in the—" She got up and hit it again. Again, it was like hitting one of those oak trees.

"So that's it, that's what she was doing," Aunt Margaret said. "Propping things back there."

"Come out of there, boy," Aunt Margaret hollered through the door. "You hear me?"

She said one of them slammed that chair against the wall again. She said she tried to vision what chair it was, but she didn't have time for visioning. She started to hit the door with her shoulder, but she thought about Tite and ran out on the gallery. Tite was still at the fence, letting the dog lick her hand. "Master," Aunt Margaret said, and ran back inside. Just about then that chair or something else heavy slammed against the wall. Then it got quiet—too quiet.

"What y'all doing?" Aunt Margaret said softly, holding her ear against the door. "Miss Louise, what y'all doing in there?"

Then she heard another loud, booming noise, like somebody had jumped from one end of the room to the other. Marcus said:

"I got you now, I got you now, you pretty little hot pretty thing. I got you now, hanh? Hanh? Give me my two little pears here. Give 'em here. Give me my two little sweet pears."

Aunt Margaret said she hit that door with all her might, but again it was like hitting that oak tree. She fell and got up and hit it again: this time it was like hitting that oak tree with another tree behind it.

She heard a slap.

"What was that?" she called, and listened. "What was that? You slapped that white woman, boy?"

She said she heard, "Why you pretty little hot—you taking it off or I'm go'n tear it off?"

"She ain't go'n do nothing and you neither," Aunt Margaret said through the door. "Not long as I can draw breath."

She hit the door with her shoulder. She fell, got up, and ran out on the gallery to see what Tite was doing. Tite was letting the dog lick her hand, so Aunt Margaret ran back into the room.

Marcus was saying, "Lord, look how pretty you is. Lord, I didn't know you was this pretty. How can a man leave all this pretty goodness and go—Oh, Lord, look at all this. And look at my two little pears hanging here, just look at 'em."

Aunt Margaret hit the door and hit it again.

She heard Marcus saying, "Now see me, see how pretty I'm is. See that? See?"

"Boy, you naked in there?" Aunt Margaret called through the door. "You naked in there, boy?"

"Let me kiss you," he said. "Oooooo, you sweet. Good Lord—Lord, have mercy. He know you this sweet? Let me kiss this little pear here . . . now this one. Two of the sweetest little pears I ever tasted. 'Specially this one here . . . Go on touch it. That's right, touch it. Won't hurt you. See? See?"

Aunt Margaret hit the door again. She hit it again, again, again. Then she heard him laughing. She figured he was carrying Louise to the bed, because the next sound she heard was the spring when they laid down. She pushed against the door again—not with her shoulder—with both hands. But she knew it was no use. And even if she had got into the room, it would have been too late now. She could tell by the deep moan that Louise made.

She turned now and went outside to pull Tite away from the fence. While she led Tite across the yard, Tite raised her other hand and showed her a nickel. Aunt Margaret didn't say anything, she couldn't say anything; she started crying when Tite wasn't looking. She sat down against one of the big oak trees and pulled Tite in her lap.

# 33

Aunt Margaret didn't know how long she sat there. She was facing the house and crying. Tite had gone to sleep in her lap. She passed her hand over Tite's head. Tite's hair was white like cotton and it felt like rabbit fur. It wasn't much longer than rabbit fur, either.

Aunt Margaret looked at the house again. The house was quiet—too quiet. The yard was too quiet; the whole plantation was too quiet.

"It won't end good," Aunt Margaret thought. "It's all right for the others, the ones in Baton Rouge—yes, it's all right for them. They have the right to do what they doing. Everybody expect them to do it. It was done from the start and it will always be done. But this won't end good. Even if she don't tell him, it won't end good. He go'n pay, she go'n pay, both of them go'n pay for this day."

When Louise first came off the bayou from around Lake Charles, she didn't know anything. She didn't know where she was, she didn't know who she was, she hardly knew why she was here. She was fifteen then—that was ten years ago—but she acted like somebody eight or nine. She acted like a week-old calf that was led to a new pasture. Aunt Margaret

was brought up to the house to help her with the house-
work. But most of the time it was like talking to a crazy
person; she wasn't listening to anything, Aunt Margaret said.

Louise tried to run away. But each time she left, Bonbon
brought her back. One time her papa and two brothers
brought her back. Aunt Margaret said the papa had a red
face and big ears and a big nose. His teeth were yellow from
chewing tobacco. Both of his sons were just like him; both
short, powerfully built fellows. Both chewed tobacco, and
one had a half quart of wine in his back pocket. He wore
overalls and a jumper and clodhopper shoes just like his
papa and his other brother did. He took out the bottle and
handed it to his papa, and his papa unscrewed the cap and
took a swallow and passed it to the other son, the oldest one.
The oldest son took a drink and wiped his mouth and passed
it back. The younger son, before drinking, handed the bottle
toward Bonbon. Bonbon shook his head, and the young son
drank and capped the bottle and stuck it back in his pocket.

"Next time she try that you beat hell out her," the papa
said to Bonbon. "You hear me up there, Louise?"

Aunt Margaret said the papa and brothers and Bonbon
were standing in the yard, and she and Louise were standing
on the gallery. Louise went inside the house and Aunt Mar-
garet followed her.

"I beat hell out her, she try that again," Aunt Margaret
heard the papa saying. "That bottle, Jules."

Louise didn't try to run away any more. She stayed to her-
self and hardly spoke to Aunt Margaret or Bonbon. Bonbon
didn't mind because by then he was spending most of his
time in Pauline's bed, anyhow. Seven years after Louise was
there she had a little girl. The baby had come too early and
she weighed only four pounds. Aunt Margaret said from the
moment Louise saw Tite, she couldn't think of anything

else but revenge. Bonbon would have to pay. Pay for the suffering she had gone through while he slept in Pauline's bed; pay for the suffering she had gone through on that bayou with her brothers and papa.

But Louise didn't know how to get revenge. She didn't have any idea what she was going to do, Aunt Margaret said. She was twenty-two now, had given birth to a child, but she was still a child herself. She hadn't learned anything about being a woman from her papa and brothers (nobody knew for sure if her mama was alive or dead) and Bonbon hadn't taught her anything, either. So she didn't know how a woman got revenge. She knew that men shot each other, beat each other, knifed each other, but what could a woman do.

She watched Pauline. She liked Pauline, she hated Pauline. She liked Pauline's clothes, she liked Pauline's hats, she liked the way Pauline walked. She looked at Pauline the way a young girl looks at a grown woman she admires. Sometimes she even tried to walk the way Pauline did.

But she hated Pauline, too. Not because she wanted Pauline to give her back her husband; she didn't want her husband. She wanted to be free of her husband. But she knew she never would be free of him. If Pauline was white, then everything would be different. Bonbon would marry Pauline and she would be able to leave. But Pauline was not white, and there couldn't be any marriage. Since there couldn't be any marriage and since she couldn't run away without them bringing her back, then she had to find another way to be free.

So she watched Pauline, and she watched the twins that went by the gate. There was no mistaking about the children, they were Bonbon's. They were her daughter's brothers, but nothing like her daughter. They had all the life, Tite had none. But by watching them and by watching Pauline,

Louise knew how she would get her revenge. Only she didn't know if she could go through with it. She would have to practice awhile, she would have to build up her courage. Not that she was afraid of Bonbon. Bonbon couldn't hurt her any more than her papa and her brothers had already hurt her on the bayou. Physical hurt didn't matter any more. No, what she needed courage for was to put herself in a man's way to make him look at her. Because, Aunt Margaret said, she didn't know if she had anything worth looking at. Since Bonbon never looked at her, she wasn't too sure anybody else would look at her, either. So she had to build her courage, she had to practice awhile. She probably stood before the looking glass hours on hours, looking at herself; probably twisting one way, then the other, looking at herself from different sides, wondering if anybody would come. She probably put on her clothes, laid across the bed to rest a while, then got back up, took off her clothes, and looked at herself in the glass again.

Then she put it to the test. She started sitting on the gallery watching. If she got the right look she was going to make her move. She didn't care if he could or he couldn't, she just wanted him to touch her. She wanted a mark on her flesh. She had to have proof, she had to have a mark. You had white women who had just said it and had had a nigger lynched; you had some who had dreamed it and had had a nigger lynched; others had done it themselves and had had a nigger lynched; but Louise needed the mark. Because she wasn't sure she had anything worthwhile, and she was afraid if she hollered rape everybody might laugh at her. But with a mark, Bonbon would definitely have to kill the nigger. Marshall Hebert would definitely get rid of Bonbon for the stealing that he had been doing—and she would be free to leave.

Aunt Margaret sat back against the tree with Tite in her arms. Tite was still asleep; Aunt Margaret could feel her breathing.

Aunt Margaret looked at the house again. The house was quiet. The yard was quiet. Not a bird was singing in any of the trees; not a dog was barking anywhere in the quarter.

"But now it ain't rape," Aunt Margaret was thinking. "Because I was there and I know 'bout the dresser behind the door. But even if it ain't rape, if she say he touched her, won't they still kill him? Ain't he just as dead now as he go'n ever be, even if they don't kill him till next week or next year? It's when she get ready for it to happen, it go'n happen."

Aunt Margaret saw Louise come out on the gallery and go around the house. She called the dog and held him by the collar. Marcus climbed out the window and the dog growled and tried to break away from Louise. When Marcus crossed the fence, Louise turned the dog loose and went back inside. Tite had woke up, and when she saw Marcus coming across the yard, she jumped out of Aunt Margaret's lap and ran toward him. Marcus took her by the hand and led her back to the pile of leaves. Aunt Margaret was there now. She didn't say anything to Marcus, she just stood there a while, looking at him. He picked up his rake and watched her from over his shoulder. Tite picked up her branch.

"Coo-dee," she said to Aunt Margaret. "Coo-dee. You in the way."

# 34

We got back to the quarter just after dark. Bonbon's yard was red. I didn't know what it was at first; then I remembered Marcus had to burn the leaves after he raked them up. When we went by the house I saw him standing against the fire. The whole yard and the front part of the house was lit up.

Bonbon took me and Pauline home and went back up the quarter. Aunt Margaret said when he came into the yard, he stood on the walk looking at Marcus a while before he came up to the house.

"Still here, Margaret?" he said to her.

"Yes sir," she said.

He went in the kitchen and washed his face and hands and sat down at the table. A minute later Louise and Tite came out of the bedroom. Louise wore a pink dress with a black patent-leather belt round her waist. She wore sandals—not shoes; she never wore shoes. Tite had on a little blue dress with a white collar and white lace on the sleeves.

"Van-wah," Bonbon said to Tite.

Tite went to him and he picked her up and sat her on his knee. He looked at her and passed his hand over the side of her face and her hair. Her hair looked whiter still with his big red hands going through it, Aunt Margaret said. Bonbon and Tite exchanged a few words in Creole, then he kissed her and put her back on the floor. He watched Tite go back to her chair. Aunt Margaret said she never saw a father who loved his child more than Bonbon loved Tite at that moment.

Bonbon and Louise looked at each other and Bonbon said something under his breath. Louise didn't say anything; she sat down at the table and waited for Aunt Margaret to serve them. Aunt Margaret put the food on the table and moved back near the stove.

They ate quietly. Aunt Margaret was looking at Louise all the time. She wasn't worried about Louise telling—she knew Louise wasn't going to tell from the moment Louise came out in the yard to hold the dog back; she was looking at Louise to see what change this had made, if it had made any change at all.

Louise raised her head and looked at Bonbon. After a while Bonbon looked back at her. He said something about New Orleans. Louise didn't say anything; her face was as plain as a piece of blank paper. Bonbon glanced at his little girl and looked down at his food again. Louise looked at Bonbon a moment longer, then she looked at Aunt Margaret. Her face showed no more expression than it did when she was looking at Bonbon.

"Wait now," Aunt Margaret thought. "Wait now, wait. Maybe he can't see anything. Maybe you need one of them loud-speakers to make him know you been bouncing on that bed all evening, but I heard you, remember?"

Louise chewed her food slowly and looked at Aunt Margaret. Her expression didn't change.

"Wait now," Aunt Margaret thought. "Wait now. You trying to tell me you don't know what you did?"

Louise turned to Bonbon.

"Hot in New Orleans?" she said. But she looked down at her plate before Bonbon could answer her.

Bonbon glanced up at her and grunted. Louise looked up at him again after he had lowered his head. She was chewing her food slowly; her face hadn't changed.

"Wait now," Aunt Margaret thought. "Wait now—now wait. You got that much control, you, to pretend that nothing happened? Wait now." Then she thought: "Yes, yes, I see, something did happen. You nothing but a girl, and a boy come to play with you. You got tired painting your toenails and looking through that old magazine; you wanted a boy to come play with you. He come, he jumped through that window and he run'd you all over that room, and when he caught you he took you to that bed, and he made you forget everything because that was the first time a boy had ever did that to you. Oh, another one had got on you (Tite there to prove that) but he hadn't jumped through the window to get on you, he hadn't run'd you all over the room to get on you, he hadn't teared your clothes off, called them two little titties sweet little pears. But this one did, and because he did, did you forget the plan you had in mind? Is that all you wanted was for somebody—black or white—to tear your clothes off and say your titties looked like sweet pears? Or is that it until you get tired of him—because children do get tired. Or is that it until they catch y'all together or until you remember all the hurt you done suffered? What is it? What is it? Don't tell me that that fool out there can wipe away everything that easy—things you been planning ever since you been here. And how long you think this can go on before your husband find out? Do you know what you doing? Do you know? I done heard the screaming of lynching, and it's no pleasant sound, I 'sure you."

Without changing expression at all, Louise looked down at her plate again. Aunt Margaret looked at Bonbon.

"When you leave, Margaret, tell him to go," Bonbon said.

"Yes sir," Aunt Margaret said.

"Can I see the fire, Papa?" Tite asked in Creole.

"Go with Margaret," he said.

Tite slid away from her chair. Aunt Margaret took her by the hand and led her in the front room. After putting on her big yellow straw hat that she had worn up the quarter that morning, she led Tite out in the yard. The fire had died down, but still there was enough left to light up a part of the yard. Aunt Margaret could see Marcus leaning on the rake, gazing down at the fire. Tite broke away from her and ran toward Marcus. Marcus looked down at Tite and smiled at her, then he started watching Aunt Margaret from over his shoulder.

"I ain't the one to watch," Aunt Margaret said. "I ain't go'n do you a thing. He say you can go home. That's if you don't feel like jumping through that window again."

"I'm ready to leave."

"You quite sure?" Aunt Margaret said. "He look tired and sleepy, you won't have to worry 'bout him. Just another nickel for Tite."

"Kess-coo-sey?" Tite said.

Nobody answered Tite. Aunt Margaret and Marcus were still looking at each other. Aunt Margaret wanted to hit him, but she knew it wouldn't have been any use.

Marcus raked up the few leaves that laid round the edge of the fire. When the fire had burned down again, he leaned the rake and broom against one of the trees and went out of the yard. As Aunt Margaret started toward the house with Tite, she saw Louise standing in the door. Louise was watching Marcus go out of the yard.

Aunt Margaret told me all this later that night while we sat in the kitchen at the table. The longer she talked, the madder I got. I already saw myself walking into that room and busting Marcus in his mouth. And I wanted him to swing back so I could really beat the hell out of him.

"And the ones in Baton Rouge?" Aunt Margaret said. She sat close to the table, leaning on it with her hands clasped together.

I told her about Pauline and Bonbon in Baton Rouge.

"Look like you went to that saloon much as I went to that door," she said.

I nodded. Then I thought, "Hit Marcus for what? Why hit Marcus? Didn't I play the pimp? Didn't I drink with them? Didn't I find the place so he could go in and lay with her? Why hit Marcus?

"Hit him because you know what can happen, that's why," I thought. "Because you know they have no pity when they come for one, that's why. Hit him because if they found out about him, every man, woman and child's life would be in danger, that's why."

I stood up to leave.

"You ate supper?" Aunt Margaret asked me.

"I'm not hungry, Aunt Margaret. Thanks."

I thought about one thing when I left Aunt Margaret's house: going home and busting Marcus in his mouth. But before I got halfway there I had changed my mind again. Because I knew that this wouldn't stop Marcus. Nothing was going to stop him. Nothing could stop him unless you killed him or locked him up in prison. I was hoping that when his trial came up they would lock him in prison, but after thinking about it I knew that wasn't going to happen. Not after Miss Julie Rand had given Marshall Hebert's people forty years of her life.

When I came to the house, instead of going to Marcus's room I went to my own room. I opened up a bottle of beer and drank half of it, then I threw the bottle out of the door. I went back on the gallery, grinding my fist in the palm of my hand. I don't know how many times I went from one end of the gallery to the other before I went in the room where he was. He was laying on the bed in the dark. I went to the bed and stood right over him. He didn't move, he didn't even look at me.

"When they come after you, Marcus, don't come to me," I said, calmly as I could. "Don't come to me, because I won't hide you."

He didn't even look at me. My fist was clenched, but I knew I wasn't going to hit him. I only hit people to protect myself or to protect somebody else. But to hit Marcus was just a waste of time.

# 35

We didn't have any more to say to each other after that. He stayed on his side of the house, I stayed on mine. He stayed on his side of the gallery, I stayed on mine. There wasn't any dividing line on the gallery—no wall, no fence or anything like that—but there was a board on the floor neither one of us was crossing. When he got hungry he went up to Mrs. Laura Mae to eat. Whether he washed his hands and face up there I can't tell, but he wasn't using my washpan and tub any more. I didn't tell him not to use it, I didn't care if he did or not; but since we weren't speaking to each other, he took it for granted I didn't want him using any of my things.

Monday, in the field, I didn't have any pity on him. I drove the tractor just like I was supposed to drive it when three people were working back there. When he fell back I threw him a sack that I had brought from the yard. When Freddie, John and I got to the end we rested. When Marcus caught up, I drove off again. John and Freddie didn't know what to make of it. They could tell that Marcus and I had had a run-in, but they couldn't tell what it was about.

But working Marcus like a mule no more changed him than Murphy's one punch or Bonbon's riding that horse six inches behind his back. He went up the quarter with me at twelve, laying flat on that corn and looking for her just like he had done all the other times. And she was there, too. She was sitting in that chair with one leg tucked under her (like a child ten or eleven), waving a piece of white rag over her shoulders like she was shooing away flies. I didn't know until later that this signal was to let him know what days he could come there and what days he couldn't.

Tuesday at one, when Aunt Margaret knocked off, Louise told her to come back the next evening. Aunt Margaret said since she worked Tuesday, Thursday, and Saturday mornings, she couldn't imagine why she had to go back Wednesday. She didn't say anything then, but Wednesday around four thirty she went back up there and asked Louise what she had to do.

"Take care Judy," Louise said.

Aunt Margaret still didn't know why all of a sudden on Wednesday (and in the evening, too) she had to look after Tite. She and Tite sat on the gallery a while, then they walked across the yard under the big trees. They even went out to the store and bought cold drinks and stood on the gallery watching the sailboats on the river.

But inside the store, just before they went out on the gallery, old Godeau, the clubfoot Cajun storekeeper, had given Tite a penny stick of peppermint candy. He always gave Tite a penny candy or a penny gum when she came to the store because he knew she had a bad heart. After handing her the candy, he looked at Aunt Margaret. Aunt Margaret was shaking her head sadly.

"Maybe he give his wife little bit more, that black one down there little bit less, this one don't come like that," old Godeau said.

"I don't know nothing 'bout that," Aunt Margaret said, and led Tite out on the gallery.

When they finished drinking their cold drinks, they took the empty bottles back inside and told old Godeau good day. But as they went back on the gallery, Aunt Margaret stopped Tite and asked her if she had told old Godeau thanks for the peppermint candy.

"No," Tite said.

"Go back in there and say, 'Maa-cee boo-coo, Monshoo Godeau'; then come on back out here."

Tite went back into the store. "If I don't tell the poor little thing how to act, she'll never know," Aunt Margaret thought. "God knows them two down the quarter don't ever teach her nothing." Tite came back.

"You told him?" Aunt Margaret asked her.

"Wee," Tite said.

They went back down the quarter and sat on the gallery. While Bonbon, Louise and Tite were eating supper that night, Bonbon told Louise he had to go somewhere later on. Louise glanced up at him but didn't say anything. What could she say? Bonbon had been going somewhere after supper two and three times a week for the past ten years. After he left, Aunt Margaret and Tite went out on the gallery to sit down. They hadn't been out there five minutes when they heard the dog growling on the left side of the house. Aunt Margaret looked toward the road, but she didn't see anybody passing by. The dog growled again. "Something in this yard," Aunt Margaret thought. She got up and went to the end of the gallery, still holding Tite by the hand. She said she had expected to see another dog or a cat outside the fence—but who did she see?

Marcus was standing outside the fence, looking up at

Louise's bedroom window. Aunt Margaret made a loud groan and nearly fell down on the gallery. But she managed to get Tite back before Tite could see him. She led Tite back to the chair and sat down.

Louise went out the back door to lead the dog away. The dog growled and growled, Louise pulled and pulled. Aunt Margaret couldn't see them, but she could tell from the dog's growling that he was straining to get to Marcus, and Louise was straining to get him away from the fence. Louise won out. A moment later Aunt Margaret heard the fence sagging and saw it shaking as Marcus climbed over into the yard. Then Louise came back inside—and the same noise from last Saturday started all over again. Looked like they kept picking up that same chair and slamming it against the wall, Aunt Margaret said. Then looked like they pulled out a dresser drawer and slammed that on the floor, then looked like they both jumped on the bed at the same time (feet first), then jumped down at the same time. Then one of them, or maybe both of them, picked up that chair and slammed it against the wall again. "Like she was trying to make up for all the playing she had never had," Aunt Margaret said.

"Mama kill rat?" Tite said.

"Yes."

"I want see rat."

"He might bite you, honey. He's a big old rat," Aunt Margaret said.

Then the slamming and falling and jumping stopped. It was quiet now. But not quiet either—because now the spring on the bed started, Aunt Margaret said.

A half hour later, Louise came out the room and went out in the yard again. Aunt Margaret said no sooner Marcus hit the ground, the dog started growling. And it was a good thing Marcus was still nimble at getting over fences because the dog got away from Louise a couple seconds before he was supposed to.

Louise came back inside and out on the gallery where Aunt Margaret and Tite were sitting.

"You can leave, Margaret," she said.

"Yes'm," Aunt Margaret said, looking up at her, but not moving.

Louise's yellow hair stood frizzly on her head. Her blouse was half buttoned and her skirt wasn't straight. Aunt Margaret said Louise was standing so close to her she could smell the sweat on her body—"the remanents of they tussling."

"And when must I come back?" she asked.

"Come, Judy," Louise said.

"How long, Miss Louise, 'fore you holler rape? How long?"

"Come, Judy."

Tite slid away from Aunt Margaret.

"Bon-swa, Mar-greet."

"Give Margaret a kiss, baby," Aunt Margaret said.

Tite kissed her. Aunt Margaret held her a moment against her bosom. While she was holding Tite she looked up at Louise.

"Think of your child," she said. "Trouble can only hurt her."

"Come, Judy," Louise said.

# 36

Aunt Margaret came down the quarter and told me about it that night. I was sitting on the gallery strumming my guitar. Marcus had gone into his room only a minute or two before Aunt Margaret came down there. After she left, I sat there gazing out at the darkness. All around me was black—black and quiet. Crickets were chirruping in the grass but they just made things quieter. I could hear my heart thumping in my chest. I squeezed my fist tight and I could hear my knuckles cracking. I looked at the door to Marcus's room and I slammed my fist in the palm of my hand. My fist sounded like a rifle shot. I sat out on the gallery by myself until way past midnight. The quarter was even quieter than it was at first, because now I was the only person still sitting up.

Friday evening when I was getting ready to go back in the field, I saw Aunt Margaret coming down the quarter. She wore a white dress and a big yellow straw hat. That dust in the road was nearly white as her dress. Before Aunt Margaret got to me, I knew what she had to say was going to be about Marcus and Louise. I was about to crank up the tractor, but I thought I ought to wait. She came up to me sweating and breathing hard. She hadn't been walking more than a couple minutes, but that sun was so hot it had taken away her breath. She told me she had to go back up the quarter that evening. A little boy had brought her word from Louise. Louise had paid the boy a nickel.

"Do you know what's going to happen when he catch him up there and you up there, too?" I asked her.

"I know," she said.

"Then why go up there, Aunt Margaret?"

"How 'bout that child?"

"Let her look after herself."

Aunt Margaret looked at me a long time (only old people can look at you like that when they think you've said something wrong), then she started shaking her head.

"That ain't you speaking, James," she said.

"It's me," I said.

"No, it ain't you," she said.

She still looked at me a long time: only old people can look at you like that.

"I see," I said. "You want me to stop him. How? Kill him? Kill him and serve his time, is that it?"

"I didn't ask you to kill nobody, James," she said, looking at me from under that big yellow straw hat.

"You want me to stop him, though," I said. "You want me to stop him before Bonbon catch him up there. How if not kill him—pray and stop him?"

"You don't have to blaspheme the Lord, either, James," she said, looking at me from under that big yellow straw hat.

"All right," I said, "I won't blaspheme Him any more. I won't even think about Him—either Marcus."

I cranked up the tractor. A minute later I saw John and Freddie coming down the quarter. Marcus slid off the gallery and came out of the yard, too. He wore a pink shirt and blue pants. Since we had stopped talking to each other, he had stopped wearing my khakis. He had on a thin beige cap. The cap had a pair of dark shades connected to the bill, and Marcus had the shades over his eyes.

Marcus got in the trailer and leaned back against the side with his arms folded. He looked like somebody going to a picnic instead of a person going out in the field. John and Freddie got in the other trailer. They looked at Marcus and said something to each other, but not loud enough for anybody else to hear. I doubt if Marcus had exchanged a half dozen words with them all the time he had been working out there.

"Well, I'm taking off," I said to Aunt Margaret. The tractor was making so much noise she could hardly hear me. "My advice to you is stay from up there."

"That's not you talking, James," she said, looking at me from under that big yellow straw hat.

"Do like you want," I said.

I swung up on the tractor and started in the field.

Five minutes after Bonbon left that night, the dog started growling. Aunt Margaret was sitting out on the gallery with Tite in her lap. She didn't bother to look to the side; she knew what she would find there, anyhow. The dog growled one minute, two minutes, maybe three—and Louise still hadn't gone outside to pull him from the fence.

"Why?" Aunt Margaret thought. "She got enough already—or is Bonbon coming back."

The dog growled.

"Wait," Aunt Margaret thought. "Now I know what she doing. She watching him from that window. She probably laughing her head off at him right now. She want him—yes, she want him, but she go'n tease him a while. She go'n show him he can't get a thing both of them want him to get till she get ready for him to get it."

The dog growled.

"Possum?" Tite said.

"A rat," Aunt Margaret said, holding Tite close.

When Louise had laughed at Marcus all she wanted to (at least this is what Aunt Margaret thought she was doing), she went out in the yard and pulled the dog from the fence. Aunt Margaret heard the fence sagging as Marcus climbed over in the yard. But soon as he hit the ground, the dog got away from Louise and started after him again. Then Aunt Margaret heard the loud, booming noise as Marcus jumped through the window into the room. From the sound of things he hadn't beat the dog by more than an inch.

Louise came back inside and the noise started all over again. Only this time it was much worse than it was last Wednesday or last Saturday. Looked like the whole place was coming apart, Aunt Margaret said. Looked like they overturned both the dresser and the armoire at the same time. Looked like Louise crawled under the bed and Marcus crawled under there after her; then halfway under he decided to stand up with the bed on his back and slam it against the wall.

"I wonder if that fool beating that woman for letting that dog get his shoe heel," Aunt Margaret thought.

"Ma-ma kill rat?" Tite said.

"Not yet," Aunt Margaret said, holding her close.

Then Louise broke out of the room and ran out in the back yard. Marcus was right behind her; then Aunt Margaret heard him throwing on brakes. Because, Aunt Margaret said, much as he wanted what Louise was running with, he didn't want it bad enough to run out in that yard where nobody was holding that dog. Tite wanted to go inside to see the big rat, but Aunt Margaret held her close.

"He might bite you," she said. "And Margaret won't like that."

Louise stood out in the small yard a while, then Aunt Margaret heard the back gate slamming. "She's in the big yard now," Aunt Margaret thought; "he's still in the house, and that dog is between them. Now if Bonbon come, all he got to do is set fire to the house and stand out there with that gun just in case this one try to jump through the window again."

Aunt Margaret heard the dog barking. Not barking at an enemy, barking at a friend. The barking was coming from the right, so Louise had to be standing in that direction. Marcus stood on the back gallery a while, then he moved back into the room. Aunt Margaret didn't hear him moving, but she figured (from what happened next) that's what he had done. She didn't hear him jump out of the window, either; what she heard was the dog barking viciously and moving fast to the left side of the yard. Then she heard the fence sagging as Marcus jumped on it and swung over all in one motion. Again he had beat the dog by only a fraction of an inch.

So both him and Louise were in the big yard now. For a minute Aunt Margaret didn't see or hear anything. Then she saw something that looked like a little ghost running way across the yard; a second later she saw a bigger one running after it. Louise broke around an oak tree and Aunt Margaret couldn't see her any more. But she could see Marcus. He was on one side of the tree, Louise was on the other side. The dog had broke to the front, too, but he was in the small yard and couldn't get near them. So Marcus and Louise played like squirrels around the tree—Marcus darting one way, Louise the other; then Marcus, then Louise. Tite hadn't seen them because Aunt Margaret kept Tite's head pressed to her bosom. More than once Tite tried to get out of Aunt Margaret's lap to see what was making the dog bark, but Aunt Margaret held her closer. Soon Tite started to fret, and

Aunt Margaret took her inside to give her a piece of cake.

The window was opened, so Aunt Margaret could still see Marcus and Louise in the yard. While Tite sat at the table eating cake and drinking clabber, Aunt Margaret stood at the window watching Louise and the convict. They played out there like two children who didn't have a thing in the world to hide. Aunt Margaret said Marcus ran around the oak tree, and Louise broke for the pecan tree a few feet away. Marcus ran there, and Louise ran to the oak tree again. Marcus ran there, and Louise broke across the yard. Marcus caught up with her and tripped her down, but she kicked and wiggled until she was free and running again. He jumped up, caught up with her, and tripped her again. She kicked herself free. All this time the dog was barking—running from one end of the small yard to the other end, barking. Marcus jumped up and caught up with Louise and tripped her down again. This time he kept her there. Aunt Margaret watched them tussling and rolling over and over. Then they stopped. They laid quietly, side by side, holding each other, kissing each other . . .

Aunt Margaret had put Tite to bed and was sitting on the gallery when Louise came in the small yard and led the dog to the front. Marcus came in the house through the back and went straight to the bedroom. Louise turned the dog loose and came inside, and Aunt Margaret could hear them talking quietly while they put things back in order. A half hour later, Louise came out to hold the dog, and Marcus went out through the back. He didn't run, he didn't climb the fence, he walked out through the back like he was leaving his own house. After he had gone, Louise came back through the house and out on the gallery where Aunt Margaret was sitting.

Aunt Margaret went inside to get her straw hat. She had hung it in the kitchen against the wall. So by the time she had put it on and come back in the living room, Louise was standing in the room waiting for her.

"Margaret, do you think a white girl could love a nigger?" Louise said. "I mean a nig-gro."

Aunt Margaret said she fixed her hat more squarely on her head and got out of there. She didn't bother to answer Louise.

The next day (Saturday), when we came in with the two loads of corn, Bonbon was waiting for us by the crib.

"Make it, huh?" he said to me.

"Yeah."

He looked at Marcus now. Marcus was standing 'side the trailer. He had on that beige cap with the dark shades over his eyes. He had on a blue shirt and a pair of old brown striped pants. He had on black and white pointed-toed shoes. Bonbon looked at Marcus like he was trying to figure him out. He didn't hate Marcus, he didn't have anything personal against Marcus, he just wondered what made him act the way he did.

"The old man say you done a good job for me last week," Bonbon said to Marcus. "Now he want you do a good job for him. Rake, broom—everything in the tool shop."

Marcus looked over the yard and looked at Bonbon again. He didn't mind the work at all. Or if he did, he wasn't going to let Bonbon know it.

"That's if you don't want do it, Geam?" Bonbon said to me.

I shook my head.

"You sure now?" he said, squinting at me.

"I'm sure," I said. "I'm making it on down."

"See you, Geam."

"See you later."

I walked away, he walked away; Marcus was still there.

# 37

After a while Marcus went to the store. The store was full of people, Negroes and Cajuns. The Cajuns were drinking at the little bar in back; the Negroes were making grocery at the front counter and drinking in the little side-room. Everybody looked at Marcus when he came in. Some of the Cajuns even turned around to look at him. Marcus bought his food and went back outside. His dinner was a loaf of bread, a half pound of baloney sausage, and two big bottles of cold drinks. He sat under the pecan tree to eat his dinner. The Negroes who went by the tree nodded to him, but hardly opened their mouths, and not one of them stopped to talk. The Cajuns who came out of the store or went in the store just looked at him.

When Marcus got through eating, it was about one o'clock and he went back to the yard. He looked over the yard before he went to the tool shop to get his rake and broom. He said it was a joke to even think he could rake that yard in a day, to even think he could rake all those leaves in a week. No, it wasn't the leaves they wanted done—Bonbon and his crowd wanted him to try to escape. Since it was too hot to hunt rabbits and possums now, they wanted to hunt niggers. But he wasn't running. At least, he wasn't running now. He was going to pull corn, he was going to rake leaves, he was going to do everything else they wanted him to do. Then when they had forgotten all about him he was going to make his move.

Marcus got a rake and broom out of the tool shop and started working. The whole yard was covered with leaves. There were as many leaves by the tool shop as there were anywhere else, so Marcus started raking them up soon as he came out the door.

Marcus had been working about an hour when Marshall Hebert came out on the back gallery and looked down at him. Marshall wore his seersucker suit, his panama hat, and he had a drink in his hand. He watched Marcus ten or fifteen minutes before he came down in the yard. He didn't come directly to Marcus at first, he stood back a ways looking at him. Marcus knew he was there without looking around. He had seen him on the back gallery and he had seen him coming down the stairs.

"If you one of them fat old punks, you better go mess with somebody else," Marcus thought. "I'll pull corn, I'll rake leaves, but I ain't messing with no punk—I don't care who he is."

He went on with his work. He had started to sweat. Raking leaves here was much harder than raking them in Bonbon's yard. There was too much grass here, especially the bullhead grass. Every now and then the rake got hooked in the grass and Marcus had to lean over and pull it loose.

Marshall came closer. He was standing only a few feet away from Marcus now. Still, he hadn't said anything. And Marcus hadn't looked at him since he came in the yard.

"See Mr. Sidney got you working," Marshall said.

"Yes sir," Marcus said, not looking around.

Marshall grunted. Marcus raked the leaves without looking at him. Everything was quiet for a while.

"What's your name?" Marshall asked.

"Marcus," Marcus said, without looking at him.

"Marcus what?" Marshall asked.

"Payne," Marcus said.

Then it was quiet again. Marshall could have been drinking, but Marcus wasn't sure. He went on working.

"When do you think you'll run, Marcus?" Marshall asked.

Marcus looked around now, he jerked around. Marshall was raising the glass to his mouth. When he lowered his hand, his cold blue eyes looked straight at Marcus.

"So you not a punk," Marcus thought. "So you know it, too."

"Run?" he said. "Run where?"

Marshall didn't answer him; he didn't think it was necessary to answer Marcus.

"I ain't going nowhere," Marcus said.

"Next week?" Marshall said. "Next month?"

"No time," Marcus said.

"No?" Marshall said, looking at the dark shades over Marcus's eyes.

Marcus raised his hand and moved the shades back against the bill of the cap.

"The day you want to go, you let me know," Marshall said. "I can have a car there for you. There could be money, too."

"I'm satisfied right where I'm at," Marcus said.

"Are you?" Marshall said.

He looked at Marcus from his blue shirt to his brown striped pants to his black and white, pointed-toed shoes. He knew that anybody who wore clothes like these didn't have any idea of staying in one place too long, and especially on a plantation. He looked up at Marcus's face and grunted.

"You're going to run, boy, and you know it," he said. "But you won't live to get out of this parish."

He looked at Marcus as he raised the glass to his mouth. He looked at him while he drank, and he was still looking at him when he lowered his hand.

"Ten years for killing a nigger, and you didn't even get near that pussy," he said.

"Five years," Marcus said. "And that's if I'm guilty."

"You're guilty," Marshall said. "And it's ten. Time for killing niggers just went up."

He looked away. His coat was unbuttoned and Marcus could see how his big stomach hung over the belt. Marcus thought: "One hard lick in the belly with this rake and I could have guts all over the yard."

Marshall looked at him again. He knew what Marcus was thinking.

"Not me," he said. His cold blue eyes looked straight in Marcus's face. "The man killing you in the field out there."

A blaze shot up in Marcus's body and his head and he thought he was going to fall. He started trembling so much, he had to grip the rake tighter to steady himself.

"Nobody killing me nowhere," he said, quickly and calmly as he could.

"No?" Marshall said.

"No," he said, calmly as he could.

"Give him time, he will," Marshall said.

"I guess you go'n see to it," Marcus said.

"I've got nothing to do with it," Marshall said.

Marcus felt like raising up that rake and bringing it down on Marshall's head. But he knew he would surely die if he did this. If he held out, he knew he would get away.

"I'll take my chance," Marcus said.

"Yes," Marshall said. "I'm sure you got that in mind. But you can't get away from here without help, and I'm the only man who can help you."

"That's if I kill for you," Marcus said.

"Kill for me?" Marshall said. "Who said anything about killing for me? You better watch your tongue, boy. It's not safe to talk like that. I said I would help you get away if you decided to run. I said nothing about killing for me. You can get yourself killed for talking like that. You be careful now."

They faced each other a while, then Marshall looked over his shoulder toward the crib. Marcus looked over there, too. He could see the two trailers of corn parked before the crib door. Marshall turned back to Marcus.

"Those children stay sick here lately," he said. "I wonder if it's mumps going around."

Marcus didn't say anything. He felt a big knot rising up in his throat. But he looked straight at Marshall to keep Marshall from knowing how he felt.

"You can unload that corn tomorrow," Marshall said, and walked away.

Marcus watched him raising the glass to his mouth as he went across the yard. Marcus felt his eyes burning: he was crying.

# 38

Marcus came down the quarter about seven o'clock that night. (I wasn't there, I had gone to Bayonne with Snuke and them to see that woman again. Aunt Margaret told me what time he came home.) The next day he got up about six and went to the yard to unload the corn, and he didn't come back down the quarter until around three that evening. He laid down on the gallery a couple hours, then he got up and took a whore bath at the hydrant. I was home then; I was in the kitchen ironing a pair of khaki pants on the table. I thought he was going to dress and go somewhere, but after he took his bath, he came inside and went to bed. The next morning he went in the field, and still he hadn't said anything to me. Neither one of us had said a word to each other in over a week now. When we came in for dinner, he hopped off the trailer at the house and went in the yard. This was the first time he hadn't gone up the quarter since he and Louise started looking at each other. When I went by the house, I saw her sitting on the gallery watching the tractor. When I came back down the quarter with the two empty trailers, she was looking for him again. That evening he went back in the field and pulled the sack when he got too far behind, and when he came in that night he hopped off the trailer and went in the yard. Louise was looking for him when I came up the quarter. She was standing up this time. When I was coming back, I saw her and her little girl walking across the yard. She looked at me like she wanted to ask me a question, but we didn't even nod to each other.

That same night she sent word to Aunt Margaret—"Don't come to work in the morning, come in the evening." Aunt Margaret went fishing the next morning, and that evening between four and four thirty, she went back up the quarter. She and Tite were sitting out on the front gallery when Bonbon left that night. She expected to hear the dog barking a minute or two after Bonbon had gone, but ten minutes passed and she hadn't heard a thing. A half hour, and nothing; then a whole hour, and nothing.

Aunt Margaret could hear Louise walking around in the bedroom. She went from the door to the window, from the window to the door. Then it was quiet—like she was standing at the window—then she started walking again. She came into the living room. She stayed in there a minute, then she went into the kitchen. She was in there a while, then she went out on the back gallery. Next, Aunt Margaret saw her walking across the yard. She looked small and lost under the black, moss-heavy trees, Aunt Margaret said. "Yes," she thought. "That's what it is. That's what it done come to now." Louise went to the gate. "But how?" Aunt Margaret thought. "How in the world could the Master let a thing like that happen— Ehh, Lord." Louise held on to one of the pickets in the gate and looked out in the road. Then Aunt Margaret saw her coming back to the house. Just before Bonbon was supposed to get back, Louise told Aunt Margaret she could leave. But the next day she sent word to Aunt Margaret to come back up there again that evening. Aunt Margaret went back. She sat on the gallery, waiting for the dog to bark. But the dog was more quiet that night than he had ever been before. After Tite fell asleep in Aunt Margaret's arms, Aunt Margaret put her in bed and came back on the gallery. Louise came to the front door where Aunt Margaret was sitting.

"Margaret?" she said.

Aunt Margaret looked over her shoulder at Louise. The light was behind Louise, throwing her shadow on the gallery.

"Tell him to come up here," Louise said. "Tell him he better come up here."

She went back to her room. Aunt Margaret heard her slamming the door. Aunt Margaret sat there a little while longer, then she came on down the quarter. She didn't stop by her place, she came on down to my house. I was sitting in the kitchen at the table. I offered her a cup of coffee, but she didn't want any. After she had been sitting there a while, telling me how Louise had been acting up there, then she told me what Louise had said.

"You want tell him for me?" she asked.

"He's out there on the gallery, Aunt Margaret," I said. "Didn't you tell him when you came in?"

"I can't talk to that boy," she said.

"I'm not talking to him, either," I said.

"Then you won't tell him?"

"Why does he have to know in the first place, Aunt Margaret? Can't you just tell Louise you forgot? At least that'll keep him from up there."

"And suppose she holler?"

"From what you've been saying, she's not going to holler," I said.

"How do you know?" she said.

I didn't answer Aunt Margaret. We could go on like that all night.

"All right," she said, standing up. "I'll do it. I'll do it.

Remember this when you come up to my house and want eat."

She walked away from the table. She thought I was going to stop her. She went all the way in the front room, then she came back.

"You still refuse to do it?" she said.

I didn't answer her. I was looking out of the window. It was pitch-black outside.

"Say yes or no," she said.

"I said no already, Aunt Margaret."

"Look at me when you say no," she said.

I turned to her.

"Say it now," she said.

Aunt Margaret looked so pitiful standing there, I knew I couldn't turn her down again. "There you go, James Kelly," I thought, "there you go. You're letting that soft heart of yours get you into trouble again."

"I'll do it, Aunt Margaret," I said.

I saw a great relief come on her face. She would rather do anything in the world than say one word to Marcus. She told me good night and left.

# 39

I sat at the table with my face propped in my hands. I was trying to figure a way to go to Marcus. I wanted to go to Marcus; I had been wanting to go to Marcus for the last couple days because I thought he needed somebody to talk to. But I knew before Marcus and I exchanged a dozen words he was going to say something to make me mad.

About ten minutes after Aunt Margaret had gone, I heard somebody coming in the room. I thought it was either Jobbo or Snuke Johnson. Sometimes Jobbo would come by with his harp, or Snuke would come by in his car and we would go riding somewhere. I didn't look up until the person stopped at the middle door. Then I saw it was Marcus. He still wore the pink shirt and the brown pants he had worn in the field that day. He had his cap in his hand. He had on his black and white pointed-toed shoes. The dew and grass had just about rubbed all the polish off the shoes now.

"Speak to you?" Marcus said.

"I was just getting ready to come out there," I said.

"I heard y'all talking."

"You know?"

"Yeah," he said.

I motioned toward the chair on the other side of the table. I didn't know what Marcus wanted to talk about, but I was sure it was going to make me mad. He sat down at the table. He had been out of the field two or three hours, but he still hadn't washed his hands or his face. I could see the dirt on his face and the rings of dirt around his neck. His pink shirt had brown sweat stains around the armpit and on the shoulder where he had been dragging the sack.

Marcus sat at the table fumbling with his cap. This was the first time we had sat down together in over a week. He didn't know how to start the conversation. He passed his tongue over his lips and started to say something, then he fumbled with the cap again.

"Can I have a beer—if you got one?" he said.

I had a couple bottles in the icebox. I got them out and gave him one. I sat back at the table with the other bottle.

Marcus drank and set the bottle on the table. He was still looking at the bottle instead of me. He started to say something, but he raised the bottle to his mouth again.

"We been talking," he said.

I didn't say anything. He raised his head and looked at me.

"We think we getting to like each other some," he said.

I still didn't say anything to him. Just waiting. Both of us knew he was going to make me mad.

"Maybe a lot," he said.

"I suppose you mean you and Louise, Marcus?"

He nodded. "Yeah."

"Well, what are you telling it to me for?"

"You the only friend I got, Jim."

I shook my head. "I'm not your friend, Marcus. I was stuck with you. That old lady in Baton Rouge stuck you on me. I'm not your friend."

He didn't hear a word I said. Even when I was talking I could see he wasn't listening. He raised the bottle to his mouth and set it back again.

"She want leave from here," he said. "She want me get her 'way from here."

"Then do it," I said. "There's a bus running out there twice a day."

"Guess you still mad at me, huh?"

"I'm not mad at all, Marcus," I said. "You said she want you to take her away; I said there's a bus running out there twice a day."

He looked at me awhile, then he started wiping the frost of the bottle with the side of his finger.

"We go'n need help," he said.

"Did you ask Bonbon?"

"No, but Marshall say he'll do it."

He had raised his head and he was looking straight at me because he knew how that was going to hit me. I didn't try to show it, but I could feel how warm I had got all of a sudden. My mind shot back to Saturday before last. I remembered how Marshall had looked at me when I told Bonbon I was taking Marcus a Coke. He had looked at me like he was thinking about Marcus at that moment, himself.

"What did you say, Marcus?"

"He'll help me."

We looked across the table at each other. We were so quiet now I could hear my heart beating.

"That's if I kill Bonbon for him," Marcus said, looking straight at me.

"You playing with me, Marcus?"

"He told me that Saturday when I was raking that yard."

I didn't say anything—I didn't believe it. I didn't want to believe I was hearing Marcus say it.

"He asked me when I was go'n run. I told him I wasn't go'n run. He said if I didn't Bonbon was go'n kill me in the field. If I got him first there might be a car and some money waiting."

"You're lying, Marcus."

"Why you think he bond me out? You think he care anything for my nan-nan?"

"Yes; because she told me so. She told me that night when I took you to Baton Rouge; she told me the other Sunday when she came here. Yes, I believe that's why he got you out. Yes, Marcus."

"Well, you wrong, and she wrong. He got me out to kill Bonbon. He got something 'gainst Bonbon or Bonbon got something 'gainst him, and he want Bonbon out the way." Marcus stopped and looked at me. His eyes were sad. I didn't know his eyes could get so sad. But I supposed it was like that with anybody who tried to be tough all the time. "I ain't no dog, Jim," he said. "I killed that nigger 'cause that nigger was go'n kill me. But I ain't no hunting dog to go round killing people for nobody else."

At first I didn't believe Marcus, but now I did. Because while he was talking, I was thinking about Marshall and Bonbon. I knew, from what Miss Julie Rand had said, that there was bad blood between them. And if Marshall wanted to get rid of Bonbon, what better way to do it than use Marcus to do it for him. Marcus already had the reputation for fighting, and anybody who worked around him and Bonbon could see that they didn't get along. So why not use Marcus to get rid of Bonbon. And who would believe Marcus if he said Marshall had put him up to do it.

I looked at Marcus across the table. I felt sorry for him, but I didn't want to show it. Because if what he was saying was true, there wasn't a thing I could do about it. Marshall was too big. If it was just Bonbon who wanted to hurt

Marcus, you might be able to prevent that. Bonbon was nothing but a poor white man, and sometimes you could go to the rich white man for help. But where did you go when it was the rich white man? You couldn't even go to the law, because he was the law. He was police, he was judge, he was jury.

"I don't believe you," I said. Because that was the easiest thing to say. That's always the easiest thing to say when you can't do anything about it. "No, I can't believe that," I said.

"Believe it if you want," Marcus said.

"Is that what you've been thinking about doing, Marcus?"

"I been thinking 'bout plenty things," he said. "I know now I got to get 'way from here and get 'way from here soon."

"Don't try that, Marcus."

"I can't stay here ten years, Jim."

"It's five—that's if you're guilty, Marcus."

"He say I'm already guilty and it's ten. They changed all the rules the day after I killed that nigger."

"He's just pushing you, Marcus. He's doing it to see what you'll do. If you don't bite for his bait, he'll leave you alone and try somebody else."

"It's not just him. I got to get 'way from here for myself. If I don't Jim, I'm go'n get in plenty more trouble. I know that."

"If you try this, Marcus, you'll really get in trouble," I said.

"Some people get away. You always hear 'bout people getting away."

"Most of them get caught, Marcus," I said. "And you're talking about taking Louise, too. You'll never make it."

"Sooner or later, Jim, I got to try," he said. "I got to get 'way from here."

"It won't work, Marcus," I told him again. "You'll need money, you'll need food, you'll need a car. It won't work. You'll just end up in Angola."

"I can't stay here ten years, Jim," he said. He was getting mad now and his voice was getting high. "I can't even stay here ten weeks," he said.

"You can if you make up your mind to do it, Marcus," I said. "If you try, if you try hard. And I'll be around here—I don't know how long—but I'll be here. I'll do all I can to—"

"I can't stay here," he screamed at me now. "Can't you see I can't stay here. Can't you see I ain't like that. Can't you see . . ."

# PART THREE

# 40

Five minutes after Bonbon left the house Friday night, the dog started growling. Louise went out in the yard and led the dog to the other side of the house while Marcus came in through the back door. Then Louise came up on the front gallery, passed by Aunt Margaret and Tite, and went in the room where he was.

There wasn't any noise tonight. No dresser behind the door, no armoire falling. No chairs slamming against the wall; no running, no jumping, no slapping. The room was quiet as the gallery, quiet as the yard, quiet as the whole plantation.

When Tite fell asleep in Aunt Margaret's arms, Aunt Margaret took her inside and put her to bed. Then she came back on the gallery and sat in her rocker again. Louise came out of the bedroom and went in the kitchen. Aunt Margaret heard her setting things on the stove, and she could smell the food when Louise dished it up and brought it back to the bedroom. Louise didn't latch the door or put anything behind it, and Aunt Margaret could hear them talking in there.

That was Friday night. Sunday morning Bonbon left the house early to go hunting with his brothers. Louise found out the day before that he was supposed to go hunting, and she had even sent word to Aunt Margaret then to come up there Sunday after church. Soon as church was over Aunt Margaret went home and changed clothes and went up the quarter. When she came in the yard, she found Tite sitting under one of the trees making mud pies. Tite was stirring the mud in a bowl and laying the pies out on a piece of tin in the sun. Aunt Margaret talked with her a while; then she went up on the gallery and sat down. She expected to hear the dog barking a few minutes after she was there, but half an hour went by and still the dog hadn't made a sound. Then, as she started inside to get a drink of water, she glanced toward the bedroom door. The door was opened just a little, but enough so Aunt Margaret could see there were two people laying on the bed.

"My Master, my Master," she said, and ran to the door. But just before shutting it, she opened it wider to say something to Marcus and Louise. They laid on the bed naked. Both of them laid on their backs, and Louise was in Marcus's arms. "Y'all gone stone-crazy?" Aunt Margaret said to them. "Y'all know that child out there? Y'all got no sense of shame, none at all?"

Neither one of them answered her. Louise looked at her and laid her head against Marcus's chest. Marcus passed his hand over her yellow hair.

That was Sunday. Wednesday evening Aunt Margaret had to go back again. When she got there Louise told her to make a blackberry pie. So after the dog had barked and Marcus had slipped in the house, Aunt Margaret and Tite went in the kitchen. She made an extra little pie for herself and Tite. After Tite had ate and gone to bed, she went back on the gallery and sat down. Louise came out there and told her to set two places at the table. Aunt Margaret did like she was told, and she had just finished setting the table when Louise and Marcus came back there. Marcus wore a brown silk shirt, dark brown pants, and brown and white shoes. Louise wore a pink dress with a white collar and white lace on the sleeves. Aunt Margaret stood by the stove looking at them. She said her heart started jumping. Not because she was scared, she had got over being scared; she wouldn't have been scared even if Bonbon had come and found them there. She would have stood her ground and told him, "Go on and kill me, go on and kill me. I know what I was doing was wrong, but I was doing it for your child. If you want kill me for protecting your child, then go right on and kill me." So her heart wasn't jumping because she was scared; her heart was jumping because she was mad. Mad because they knew she couldn't do a thing but what they wanted her to do. Since she hadn't told on them that first time, they knew she was guilty as they were; and now she had to go along with them no matter how she felt.

They sat down at the table and started eating. Marcus ate like he hadn't seen food in a week. Louise only picked at her food. Most of the time she was looking across the table at Marcus. She worshipped him, Aunt Margaret said.

When Marcus got through eating, he wiped his mouth with the back and the palm of his hand. Then he asked Louise for dessert.

"Margaret," Louise said.

Aunt Margaret didn't move. She didn't even look at Louise—she was looking at Marcus. She hadn't taken her eyes off him more than a second since he came in the kitchen. There was a pan of hot soapy water on the back of the stove to wash dishes in, and she had been thinking about picking it up and dumping the water on Marcus.

"Margaret," Louise said. Then she looked at Marcus again. "Want coffee with it, honey?"

He nodded.

"Margaret," Louise said.

Aunt Margaret served the pie, then the coffee. She said Marcus sucked on his tooth when she was putting the coffee before him. She started to hit him with her fist, but she knew it wouldn't have done any good. She looked down at him a moment, but he never raised his head. She moved back to the stove to watch them.

"When you going?" Louise asked him.

"Tomorrow night if he there."

"Jim going with you?"

"I doubt it."

"By yourself?"

"I guess so," he said, blowing in the coffee and sipping it.

"You taking a chance by yourself, honey," she said.

"I got to," he said. "That's the only way."

"I'm scared," she said. "If anything happen to you, Marky-poo."

"Nothing go'n happen," he said. "Long as you sure 'bout everything you told me. He been doing all that stealing 'cause Marshall can't touch him."

Louise nodded.

"And he's the only one?"

"I'm pretty sure."

"None of his brothers?"

"No."

"And nobody else?"

"I'm sure he's the only one."

Marcus nodded his head. "He probably is. Marshall couldn't take that chance if they had somebody else, too."

"You think it'll work?"

"I can go to him, tell him us proposition. If he don't want it, we just figure another way out."

"But we'll go, won't we, Marky?"

"We'll go," he said.

Louise smiled. She worshipped Marcus.

"Honey, you the bravest man in the world," she said.

"You pretty sweet, too," he said.

She smiled again, showing her teeth and her gum. Aunt Margaret had never seen her so happy before.

"Like the pie?" Louise asked.

"It's pretty good," Marcus said.

"Heard that, Margaret?" Louise said. "Maybe when we get up North we'll send for you."

"Y'all ain't going nowhere," Aunt Margaret said. "Y'all go'n die right here. 'Specially him there."

"Nobody go'n die," Louise said.

"Both o' y'all," Aunt Margaret said. " 'Specially him. Right here."

"We going, ain't we, honey?" Louise said.

"We going," he said.

"Y'all going, all right," Aunt Margaret said. "Both o' y'all going, all right. Soon's they find out, y'all sure going."

"Shut up, Margaret," Louise said.

"You go'n make me shut up, Miss Louise?" Aunt Margaret said.

"Yes, I'm go'n make you shut up," Louise said. "Shut up."

"Let her talk, honey," Marcus said. "Let her get it off her chest. We don't worry 'bout what she think. You starting to worry 'bout what she think?"

"No," Louise said.

"Y'all think y'all children," Aunt Margaret said. "Y'all think y'all making mud pies in the yard. Not a black and a white child—no, 'cause a black and a white child old enough to make mud pies already know they can't ever live together. No, y'all act like two black children or two white children playing in the yard. There ain't nothing to stop y'all from going North 'cause North right round the house. Well, North ain't right round the house, and y'all ain't no chil-dren. Y'all grown people, and y'all white and y'all black. And there ain't no North for y'all. There ain't nothing but death—a tree for him; and as for you . . ."

"Honey, come here and kiss me," Marcus said.

Louise got up and went to him.

# 41

The next evening, late, Bishop sat in the kitchen shelling dry beans. He dropped the yellow hulls and the white beans in the same pan. After he got through he was going to gather up all the hulls and put them in the trash basket back of the stove; then he was going to pour the beans in the white sack and weigh them on the little kitchen scale. He had about four pounds of beans in the sack that he had already gotten out of the garden that summer, and he figured what he was going to add tonight was going to make it close to five pounds.

Bishop heard Marshall coming down the hall toward the kitchen. Marshall was drinking bourbon and water. He went by Bishop without saying anything, and Bishop didn't say anything, either. He had been in the house over twenty years, and he knew better than to speak if Marshall was in one of his bad moods. Marshall went to the door and looked through the screen. He was so big, he nearly hid the door from Bishop. His silver-color hair was too long, his big red neck bulged over his shirt collar. Bishop looked at him and thought, "Poor man, poor man." Marshall raised the glass to his mouth; then he pushed the door open and went outside. "Wonder what that Cajun done stole now," Bishop thought. He heard Marshall going down the back stairs; then after a minute or two, Marshall came back inside again. He went by Bishop without even glancing his way. "He done stole something, I'm sure," Bishop thought. "I didn't miss any of the hogs, though. Maybe it was some more corn, or maybe one of them young steers . . ."

Bishop said Marshall hadn't left the kitchen more than ten minutes when he heard the back gate slamming. He said at first he thought it was Marshall again, but then he wondered why would Marshall go out in the yard, then come back inside, then go out in the yard again through the front, just to come back inside through the back gate. He said he told himself, "No, it can't be Mr. Marshall, it must be that Cajun." Well, if it was, he was going to go right on shelling beans and he was going to let him knock a while before he got up to see what he wanted. "And he better not walk in here, either, if I don't tell him to," Bishop was thinking. He heard him coming up the back stairs, then he heard him knocking. Bishop didn't move. He heard the knocking again—this time a little bit louder. Bishop still didn't move. He even picked up another pod of beans and shelled it. Then he started thinking maybe it wasn't Bonbon, maybe it was somebody else from the quarter. Maybe somebody from down there had taken sick and had sent somebody up here to call the doctor. Or maybe somebody was dead and somebody had come up here to telephone relatives. "But who could be dead?" he asked himself. He had gone to church last Sunday, and nobody had said anything about anybody being very low sick. He set the pan on the table and went to the door.

"Yes?" he said, pushing the door open.

He said he moved back when he saw who was standing there, because that was the last person he wanted to see. Marcus had on the same brown silk shirt, dark brown pants, and brown and white shoes he wore at Bonbon's house the night before.

"Speak to Marshall," he said.

He didn't say "Mister," Bishop said. He didn't say "Can I?" He didn't say "Is he in?" "Speak to Marshall," he said.

"Go back down the quarter, boy," Bishop said. "Please go back down the quarter."

"Nigger, Marshall in that house?" Marcus said.

"Mr. Marshall's in there," Bishop said. "He's in his library, relaxing. But please, go back down the quarter, boy. Please go."

"Tell him I'm out here," Marcus said. "He'll know."

"I will not," Bishop said, and he tried to shut the door. But Marcus had expected something like that and stuck his foot in the way. "Boy, move," Bishop said. "Move. Please move."

"Tell him I'm here."

"I will not."

He said Marcus didn't look at him like he was mad. He wasn't mad. Marcus didn't think enough of him to get mad with him.

Bishop tried to shut the door. He opened and pulled it and opened and pulled it, but Marcus's foot was still in the way. Marcus never used his hands to stop the door, he didn't even try to push his way in the kitchen; his foot did all the work.

"Maybe if I called the law," Bishop said.

"Do that," Marcus said.

"And maybe I will," Bishop said.

But he didn't go to the telephone. He said his face, his head, his body, was on fire. He said Marcus just stood there looking at him like he might hit him. No, not because he was mad; but just hit him out of devilment.

"Please move your foot and go back down the quarter before you start trouble, boy," Bishop said.

Marcus didn't answer him, just looking at him like he might hit him any moment.

Bishop tried to push Marcus's foot away from the door with his own foot. At first he pushed on it lightly; then hard; then harder. All the time, Marcus watched him like he might hit him any moment. Bishop leaned over and tried to move the foot with his hands. He said all the time he was leaning over, he could feel his face and his head and his back on fire. He said he pushed and pushed, but to no use. Just as he was about to straighten up again, Marcus drew his foot back.

"Thank you," Bishop said. "Thank you ever so much."

But Marcus wasn't looking at him, he was looking by him. Bishop turned around and saw Marshall standing there.

"I told him you was busy, sir," Bishop said. "If you go back, I think I can handle it from now on."

"Aren't you the nigger I bailed out of jail?" Marshall said, coming toward the door. He didn't even look at Bishop.

"Yes sir," Marcus said.

"You take chances."

"I tried to get him to come to you; he wouldn't."

"I'm not to be disturbed in the evening."

"I just thought we could talk 'bout the field, sir. What we was talking 'bout last Saturday."

Bishop said everything was quiet for a moment. The big white man hid the Negro boy completely from Bishop. Bishop could feel his face and head burning.

"Did we talk last Saturday?" Marshall said.

"Yes sir."

"What about?"

"Sidney Bonbon."

"You mean Mr. Sidney Bonbon, don't you?"

"Yes sir. Mr. Sidney Bonbon."

"All right, go on and talk."

"Can't we talk in private?" Marcus said.

"Come in," Marshall said.

He turned, letting the door shut on Marcus, but Marcus caught the door before it hit him in the face. Marshall had nearly gone out of the kitchen before Bishop realized what was happening.

"Mr. Marshall," he said. Marshall was still walking. "Mr. Marshall," he said, again, quickly. Marshall was still walking; Marcus was a step behind him. "Mr. Marshall," Bishop said, reaching out his hand. "Mr. Marshall, Mr. Marshall," Mr. Marshall . . ."

Neither one of them looked back at him.

# 42

I was laying across the bed Saturday evening when I heard somebody coming up on the gallery. I had been thinking about Marcus. Aunt Margaret had already told me what Marcus and Louise had been talking about Wednesday night. He had left the house the following night to go up the quarter, and I was wondering if he had gone to Marshall Hebert. I hadn't heard anything from Aunt Margaret about it, and I hadn't said anything to Marcus about it, either. But I couldn't believe that he would go to Marshall and tell him that he and Louise wanted to leave from here together. I knew Marcus was bold (or crazy), but I didn't think he was bold (or crazy) enough to take a chance like that. This is what I was thinking about when I heard somebody coming up on the gallery. When I turned my head, I saw Aunt Margaret coming in the room. She didn't knock. She had been coming there so much lately, she didn't think she had to knock any more. A step or two behind her was Bishop. I didn't know who he was at first. I had never seen him this far in the quarter before. I had seen him far as the church, but I couldn't remember seeing him on this side of the church ever since I had been on the plantation. He was a little man with a shining bald head. He wore steel-rim glasses with thick lenses. He always had on a seersucker suit or a plain white suit. Today he had on the white suit. He had taken off his white straw hat and closed up his umbrella, and now he was carrying both of them in the same hand. He had a folded pocket handkerchief in the other hand. As he came in the door, he passed the handkerchief over his bald head. I stood up when I saw him and Aunt Margaret coming inside.

"James, you know Brother Bishop," Aunt Margaret said.

I nodded to him. I didn't speak his name because I didn't think it would have been right for me to just come out and call him Bishop. At the same time, I had never heard anybody call him Mister, and it would have sounded funny to me if I said it now.

"Take these things from you?" I said.

I took his hat and umbrella and laid them on the bed. I asked Aunt Margaret if she wanted me to rest her hat, but she didn't give it to me. She didn't answer me, either, she just started fanning with it.

"Would you people care to sit down?"

Aunt Margaret started back in the kitchen. Bishop was a step behind her, wiping his face and neck with the pocket handkerchief. The pocket handkerchief was wet and dirty, and it was more gray than it was white. I followed them in the kitchen and offered them a glass of lemonade. I wanted a beer instead of lemonade, but I changed my mind and took lemonade, too. I didn't think drinking a beer around them would have looked right.

"Brother Bishop say that boy went up there," Aunt Margaret said. I thought Aunt Margaret looked mad when she first came inside the house, and now I was sure she was. She was sitting on one side of the table, and Bishop was sitting on the other side. I sat in a chair in the middle door. Both the back door and the window were wide open to let air through the house.

"Yes," Bishop said, wiping his face and neck. "He came there Thursday night."

Then he told me everything. He told me about him shelling beans, he told me about Marshall walking across the floor drinking. He told how Marshall had gone in the yard and come back inside; how he had heard the gate slamming and thought that Marcus was Marshall at first, then how he thought it might be Bonbon. All the time he was talking he was wiping his face and neck with the handkerchief.

"He just pushed his foot in there," Bishop said, looking at me. Bishop's eyes looked big behind the thick glasses. "The house his great-grandparents built. The house slavery built. He pushed his foot in that door."

Aunt Margaret sat on the other side of the table fanning with her big yellow straw hat. She was looking toward the window, not at me or Bishop. But Bishop was still looking at me. He wanted me to know what it meant for Marcus to push his foot through a door that slavery had built.

"And then?" I said.

"Mr. Marshall invited him to his library."

"He did what?" I said.

Bishop nodded, wiping his face and neck.

"Then?" I said.

"I don't know," Bishop said. "I was too put out. A few minutes later the boy left the house. I don't know anything else."

"You didn't hear them?"

"No sir, they was in the library," Bishop said. "But I'm sure it was something to do with that Cajun. I'm sure of that."

I looked at Aunt Margaret. She was fanning with the straw hat and looking toward the window. She looked like she had given up hope on everything.

"You said they had some kind of proposition?" I asked her.

"That's what they say," she said, not looking at me.

Aunt Margaret acted like she didn't want to talk, so I looked at Bishop again.

"I'm scared, Mr. Kelly," he said.

"I'm sure Marcus's not that crazy," I said.

"No?" Bishop said. "He stuck his foot in that door. That was the house that slavery built."

Bishop wanted me to understand that any black person who would stick his foot in a door that slavery built would do almost anything.

# 43

---

Bishop drank his lemonade and looked down at the sun on the floor. When we first came back there the sun had barely reached the top step; now it had crossed the step and had come about a foot inside the kitchen. Bishop was looking down at the sun like he expected to see it move if he looked at it long enough. When a bunch of flies lit on the floor in front of him he watched the flies. When they flew away, he raised his head. Aunt Margaret was quiet all the time—just waving that big yellow straw hat before her face.

"I been seeing it coming ever since that boy came there," Bishop said. "I could see it in the clothes he wore—them pink shirts, them two-tone shoes. I could see it in the way he rode on that tractor, the way he strutted across that yard. I saw the way he looked at that Cajun from the side. And Mr. Marshall saw it, too—and that's when he started watching him. Every time the boy came to the yard, he put himself in a place to watch him. He even went riding in the quarter to look for him. Not ready to speak to him—not yet—just to look at him. Then last Saturday he made his move. He stood on the back gallery a long time before he went out there where he was. I watched them from the dining room. I kept saying, 'No—Lord, please don't let him, please don't let him.' I saw how the boy jerked around when he told the boy what he wanted him to do. I had a glass in my hand. The glass fell and broke."

Bishop had spread the wet pocket handkerchief on his knee to dry out, but now he picked it up to wipe his face and neck. He looked at me long and sadly. His thick glasses made his eyes look bigger and sadder than they really were.

"He didn't get Marcus out of jail to kill Bonbon, did he?"

Bishop frowned and groaned. He started shaking his head like he never would stop. Nothing else I could say could have hurt him more than that.

"He got him out for her," he said. "For her. He got him out 'cause she came there crying. He didn't know that boy from Adam. It was his clothes, the way he walked across that yard; it was the way he looked at that Cajun: these was the things that gived him the idea. No, he didn't get him out to kill him. God knows, I wish he had never heard of that boy, or Miss Julie Rand."

Bishop looked down at the floor again. Aunt Margaret went on fanning. Everything was quiet, while I waited for Bishop to go on.

"Exactly what is it Bonbon got on Marshall?" I asked.

Bishop raised his head slowly and looked at me. He didn't like the way I said "Marshall"; I should have said "Mr. Marshall." Then he started looking at me the way Miss Julie Rand had looked at me when I asked her that same question. He didn't want to tell me what the bad blood was between Marshall and Bonbon. It would have been different if it was something just about Bonbon. Bonbon was a poor Cajun, and he would have talked about Bonbon all day. But things were a little different when they were about Mr. Marshall. At the same time, he knew he had to tell me because he needed me. He glanced at Aunt Margaret to see what she thought. Did she think it was all right to let Marshall and Bonbon's secret out? Aunt Margaret was fanning and not looking at either Bishop or me. She had given up hope. The world was crazy. If she could save Tite out of all this madness, she would be satisfied. As for Marcus and Louise, and now Bonbon and Marshall, she had given up on them. So Bishop got no help from her at all. If he wanted to tell me, then it was up to him.

"Mr. Marshall had a brother called Bradford," Bishop said. "He was a gambler, a big gambler, but he used to lose much more than he ever won. One night he lost a great deal more than he could ever pay back. He signed a letter to the man who had won the money, then he came home and packed up his clothes and left. Nobody knows where he went and nobody knows if he's living or dead. A week or so after he left, the other man showed up with the letter, claiming his money. I heard him and Mr. Marshall squabbling over the money in the library. He left without getting the money, and a few weeks later he was killed in a saloon—another gambler killed him. The place was packed full of people and there was nothing but noise and moving with people trying to get out. While all this was going on, the second man was killed, too. Bonbon was there that night. People figure he killed the second man after he had put him up to kill that other one . . ."

Bishop let out his breath like he had been holding it in a long time. I waited for him to go on.

"He been doing anything he want ever since then," Bishop said. "Mr. Marshall been trying to get him 'way from here ever since. He's offered him money, but he won't take it. He's offered other people money to get Bonbon way from here, but they won't take the money, either. Bonbon got too many brothers; and you can't spend money from the grave."

"So he makes Bonbon work Marcus like a slave so Marcus can get mad enough to kill him?" I said. "He can see how much Marcus already hates this place, and he thinks if he press him enough, sooner or later he will have to kill Bonbon . . . ?"

Bishop lowered his head. It was the truth. But Bishop couldn't ever say anything like that about Marshall Hebert. He would rather put it all on Marcus: Marcus's clothes, his strutting, his side glances at Bonbon.

# 44

We talked for a couple of hours. Bishop wanted to know what we could do to keep this from happening. That's why he had come down the quarter to see me. He felt so helpless up there in that big house, knowing all this was going on and knowing he couldn't do a thing about it. I told him I didn't know what to do. What could I do? What could any of us do? This whole thing was left up to Marcus. Marshall was only pushing him because he had somebody to push on. But I didn't think he would push too hard and too long. As for making Bonbon kill Marcus if Marcus didn't kill Bonbon, that was just to scare Marcus. Marshall wouldn't dare let Bonbon kill for him again. He was still paying off for the first killing that Bonbon had done for him.

All the time Bishop and I sat there talking, Aunt Margaret sat on the other side of the table fanning with her straw hat. The longer we talked, the madder she got. All of a sudden she jumped up and put the hat on her head.

"You leaving, Brother Bishop?" she asked.

"Yes, Sister Margaret," he said.

I moved my chair to the side to let them go by me. After Bishop had gotten his hat and umbrella off the bed, we went out on the gallery. Marcus was coming in the yard. He had on his blue shirt and black pants; he wore his cap and dark shades. Bishop and I looked at Marcus, but Aunt Margaret wouldn't. She had given up on him. All she wanted to do now was save Tite (if that was possible). Bishop looked at Marcus like he wasn't really seeing him. His mind was somewhere else—probably at the big house with Marshall Hebert. Marcus came up on the gallery and nodded to us and went in his room.

Bishop turned to me again. He had put on his hat, and now he held the umbrella and handkerchief in one hand. He held his other hand out to me. I felt how small and soft his hand was when I shook it.

"I hope I didn't take too much of your time," he said, looking very sad.

"No sir," I said, shaking my head.

"Will you talk to the boy?"

"I've talked to him already," I said. "But I'll talk again."

"If you can't stop this, Mr. Kelly, I'm afraid what'll happen to all of us," Bishop said. "That boy touch Bonbon, them brothers go'n ride."

He looked at me a long time to show me what that meant. Then he opened his umbrella and followed Aunt Margaret down the steps. He carried his handkerchief in the other hand. He started wiping his face and neck soon as he went out of the gate.

I stood at the end of the gallery watching them. Bishop looked so weak and scared walking there beside Aunt Margaret. Aunt Margaret was probably scared as he was, but she had extra strength to keep her going—extra strength she got from believing in God. Bishop went to church every Sunday, but he didn't look to God for his strength. He looked to that big house up the quarter. And right now that big house wasn't setting on very solid ground.

I stayed on the gallery a while, then I went to Marcus's room. He was laying on the bed in his shorts. We looked at each other, but we didn't say anything. I went to the window where it was cooler and turned to look at him again. He was still watching me, waiting to hear what I had to say. I didn't know what to say to Marcus.

"Something on your mind, Jim?" he said.

I just stood there looking at him. He sat up on the bed.

"Why did you go to Marshall the other night, Marcus?" I asked him.

"Tell him to get me off free," he said. "I told him to get me off free and give me that field car and some money, and I was go'n take Louise 'way from here."

I didn't believe Marcus had said this to Marshall. You see, I knew the white people around that area. Knew them pretty good. I knew if a black man had said that, he wouldn't have lived to come out of that room.

"I told him Bonbon was go'n have to come after us, and he was go'n be free of him."

I still didn't believe him.

"That's why I went there," he said.

I leaned back against the window to look at Marcus. Now I did believe him. I believed him because I remembered he had killed and it didn't mean a thing. I believed him because I remembered he had fooled that dog and jumped through that window to get to Bonbon's wife. I believed him because I remembered he had stuck his foot in that door—"that slavery had built." I believed everything Marcus said. I just couldn't understand why Marshall hadn't killed him for saying it.

"He just stood there and let you say all that?"

"He told me to get the hell out his library. But I could see he was thinking 'bout what I had said."

"He might be thinking about telling Bonbon what you had said, you ever thought about that?"

"That's the last thing he'll be thinking 'bout doing," Marcus said. "He got to get rid of Bonbon, not me. I'm a nigger, me. I ain't nothing but a nigger. Bonbon is the man."

"And you think he'll get you off free, to let you leave here with Louise?"

"He'll get me off. Might let me wait a while—try to make me sweat—but he'll get me off."

"If he get you off, how does he know Bonbon'll follow you?"

"Because Bonbon own people'll kill him if he don't. Because this is the South, and the South ain't go'n let no nigger run away with no white woman and let that white husband walk around here scot-free. Not the South."

"You think you know the South, huh?"

"I know that much 'bout it."

"How about the part where the white man let the nigger get away with the white woman, Marcus?"

"He ain't got no choice. He might not like it, but he ain't got no choice. He got to get rid of Bonbon. Bonbon done stole too much from him, and he know long as Bonbon here Bonbon go'n keep on stealing. Not that Bonbon don't have a right to steal after what he made Bonbon do. Yeah, I know he made Bonbon kill a man for him. Now, since Bonbon stealing to pay for the killing, he want somebody to kill Bonbon. Well, not this boy. I ain't killing for him, I'm making him a safe and sound deal. Get me off and I'll get her 'way from here and Bonbon'll come after us. If that suit him, all right; if it don't, fuck him; I'll find another way to get out of this hole."

"Marcus, do you want my advice about all this?"

"If you go'n say work here ten years, forget it."

"That's what I'm going to say, Marcus. Do your work and forget all these deals. They'll never work out. All you can do is make things harder for yourself and for everybody else around here."

"Things can't get harder for me, Jim. I'm a slave here now. And things can't get harder than slavery."

"The pen can be harder."

"I ain't going to no pen. That's why I got put here."

"And that's why you ought to do as well as you can."

"Be a contented old slave, huh? That's what you mean?"

"You're not a slave here, Marcus. You're just paying for something you did."

"I don't think I ought to pay for defending myself. And I ain't go'n pay for killing that country-ass nigger. Black sonofabitch ought to don't go round with pretty women if he know he can't fight."

"You trying to be funny, boy?"

"I ain't trying to be funny. I just say I ain't go'n pay for that chickenshit sonofabitch. Fuck him."

"You don't care if the whole world burn down, do you? Do you, Marcus?"

"Long as I ain't caught in the flame, Jim," he said.

I looked at him and I felt pity for him.

"Jim, why you keep arguing with me?" Marcus said. "You the only friend I got, and you keep arguing with me."

"I want you to be a human being, Marcus."

"I'm a human being. I just don't look at things the way you do. You, you want care for everybody. Me, I don't care for nobody but me. I been like that too long now to go round changing."

"That's not a good way to be, Marcus."

"I can't be no other way. Now, please, Jim, just let me 'lone. I need some rest. I'm tired."

He laid back down.

# 45

Monday, about five o'clock, Marshall Hebert showed up in the field for the first time. I looked across the field and I could see the dust about a quarter of a mile away coming down the back road. Just in front of the dust was that '41 Ford Marshall used for his field car. I looked over my shoulder at Bonbon riding horse behind Marcus. He looked across the field toward the dust, then he looked at me. I was much higher up than he was, so he looked at me so I could tell him who was coming. I didn't have to call Marshall's name, I just nodded my head. Bonbon wouldn't have heard me anyhow, because the tractor was making too much noise. He turned the horse around and started back toward the other headland. We were pulling corn on the bayou now, and there were trees on the bayou at one end of the field. The trees were mostly gum, willow and cottonwood. You had a few ash and cypresses here and there. In the morning the shade from the trees was on the water, but in the evening the shade was on the headland. Bonbon knew that Marshall was going to park under the trees instead of at the end where there wasn't any shade, and that's why he had gone back the other way. Soon as he rode away, I slowed up the tractor. John and Freddie hollered at me to speed it up, but I didn't pay them any mind. When I got to the end, I gave Marcus a couple minutes rest before I started back down the field again.

Marshall had already parked his car under the trees at the other headland. Bonbon had gotten off the horse to talk to him. I didn't like to see them that close together. I didn't think Marshall had come out there to say anything to Bonbon about Marcus—he couldn't afford that. But if that wasn't his reason, then what was it? Why wasn't he at the front sitting on his gallery drinking like he always do?

I looked back over my shoulder. The two punks were right up on the trailer, pitching corn like two machines. They knew the big boss was out there, and now they had to show off for him. Marcus was about ten feet farther behind. He was dead tired. His pink shirt was wet and sticking to his chest.

"Move up," Freddie called.

I turned to the front and looked at Marshall and Bonbon on the other headland. They were still talking. Bonbon held the bridle reins in one hand, and he was leaning on the car, talking to Marshall through the window.

The tractor *putt-putt-putted* on toward the headland. I didn't feel good about seeing Marshall out there at all. I had a tightness in my chest. It came there soon as I saw that car headed in this direction.

"It's probably nothing," I told myself. "He's probably asking him how long it's going to take us to finish that corn. He want us to hurry so we can get into that hay before the bad weather. So stop being such a coward; stop it. . . ."

When I came up on the headland, Marshall drove the car closer to the tractor. I nodded to him, but he didn't see me; he was already looking toward the back of the trailer. When Marcus finished out his row and came to the side of the trailer where the car was parked, I could see how Marshall started watching him. Marcus spoke, but Marshall didn't answer. He had something in his mouth, probably a piece of candy, that he moved from one side of his mouth to the other. Every time his mind shifted from one thing to another, that piece of candy moved around in his mouth, too.

"How much you got, Geam?" Bonbon asked me.

He had led the horse up to the car again. He was standing a little to the front of the door where Marshall was sitting. He had made the horse turn so the horse wouldn't stand between Marshall and the tractor. In this way I could see everybody. I could see Bonbon, I could see Marshall; and if I dropped my eyes a little, I could see Marcus against the trailer. I looked back at the corn in the trailer. It was about two foot from the top.

"Almost full," I said.

"When you get back to the other end, hitch up and knock off," Bonbon said.

"Right," I said. "Freddie, one of y'all, go get the water jug."

Freddie started up the headland. The jug was under one of the trees down by the water. When we pulled corn on the bayou, we always kept the jug close to the water where the ground was cooler. Before Freddie had gone ten feet, his girlfriend John had caught up with him. Then both of them went up the headland, giggling. Bonbon squinted at them, and I looked at them, too. I don't think Marshall ever did; I don't think he took his eyes off Marcus a second after Marcus came to that side of the trailer. Now he said something to Bonbon. Bonbon started looking at Marcus, too. But he didn't look at Marcus in his usual hard way. He had quit that. Now, when he looked at Marcus, it was like he was trying to figure him out. He wanted to know why Marcus wore a pink shirt and brown pants when everybody else wore khakis; why he wore the cap when everybody else wore a straw hat; why he wore the black and white, low-cut shoes when everybody else wore brogans. Maybe Bonbon already knew why Marcus did this. This was Marcus's way of showing how much he hated the place. The only trouble was nobody was getting hurt by it but himself. After studying Marcus from head to foot, Bonbon looked up the headland.

A slight breeze stirred the leaves over our heads. The breeze hit me on the left side where my shirt was a little damp, and a cold glass of beer couldn't have pleased me more. When Bonbon felt the breeze, he took off his straw hat and passed the flat side of his wrist over his forehead. He kept the hat off a second longer so the breeze could blow through his hair. I don't think the breeze hit Marshall inside the car. If it did, he didn't show it. He was looking at Marcus all the time.

"No, it wasn't corn and hay that brought him out here," I thought. "It wasn't corn and hay at all. . . . Now I had good reason for feeling that tightness in my chest."

After the breeze had blown away, Bonbon stuck his hat back on and looked across the field where we had been working. His back was slightly turned to Marshall, so Marshall looked at him now. But from his face, you wouldn't have thought he had anything against Bonbon. His face didn't show any hatred at all. If you didn't know what was going on, you would have thought he was contented with his overseer.

Marshall shifted the piece of candy in his mouth. He was looking at Marcus again; and Marcus was looking back at him now. But he wasn't just looking at him, he was staring at Marshall. "Well?" he was saying. "You made up your mind about that car and that money?" And Marshall was saying back to him, "If I told him you went through that window, he would kill you before you moved from that trailer." Marcus said back, "You ain't go'n tell him nothing. And me and you both know you ain't go'n tell him nothing, don't we?"

I can't read minds, but if eyes could talk, this is what Marcus and Marshall were saying to each other.

John and Freddie came back and Freddie handed me the jug and we started back down the field. But just before we did, this is what happened. Marcus walked up to about arm's reach of the car and stared down at Marshall's face. Bonbon didn't see this because he was getting back on the horse. John and Freddie didn't see it either because they were on the other side of the tractor. The only reason I saw it was because I thought they had to say something to each other after they had been looking at each other like that. When Marcus walked up to the car, Marshall stared right back at him. Then he moved his head a little to the side and spit the piece of candy out of the window. It might have touched Marcus's pants leg, but I'm not sure.

# 46

Marshall was out there the next evening. We had finished that patch of corn and we had crossed the ditch into the other patch. We were still working on the bayou, though, and we still had the shade on the headland in the evening. Marshall parked the car under one of the willow trees to watch us. The limbs on the willow hung so low, the leaves brushed against the top of the car. When Marshall drove away, the leaves brushed against the top of the car again. You could see the scratch marks they left in the dust that had settled on the car.

Marshall was out there the next day. He was out there the day after that and every day for the rest of the week. He never said anything to anybody but Bonbon. And they only talked when the rest of us were down the field. When everybody was on the headland, Marshall spent most of the time looking at Marcus.

Every evening when we came in I talked to Marcus. I told him how I felt, how I didn't trust Marshall. But, of course, Marcus had to have an answer.

"I asked him for a lot of money," he said. "For a hundred dollars—and that car. He got to think about it before he make up his mind. I can understand."

Then he would take a bath and put on some clean clothes and go up to Louise. If Bonbon was home, he would go up to the church and look through the window. The next evening Marshall would show up in the field again and he and Marcus would stare at each other again. Sometimes it went on a minute, sometimes only a couple seconds. But if you knew it was coming, you would see it every time.

Why Bonbon didn't get suspicious to something going on, I don't know. Then I think I do. Bonbon had been taking from Marshall so long he had forgot it was wrong. He just couldn't see Marshall doing him anything now. He thought Marshall had accepted this as part of life, just like he had accepted taking as part of life. I say taking—not stealing—because I don't think Bonbon felt he was stealing any more. He was just taking things that Marshall was going to die and leave. There was enough there for everybody, and he didn't see anything wrong with taking a little of it. How could Marshall see anything wrong with it, either?

Every evening now when I came up to the front, I saw Bishop. He was either standing out on the back gallery or he was somewhere in the yard. He would have on his white suit or his seersucker suit, and he always had a basket on his arm. He used the basket for carrying everything from grocery from the store to clothes from the clothesline. Bishop and I never said anything to each other when I came to the yard because he never came close enough for me to speak to him. He just watched me from far off. It looked like he wanted to hear what I had to say, but he was afraid that it might be bad news. Before he would hear bad news, he wouldn't hear any. So he just stood back and watched me. If I waved at him, I would notice how that white straw hat made a little bow. A minute later if I looked for him, he wouldn't be there. Then the next day I would see him again. Usually it was dusk when I came up there, and Bishop dressed all in white looked like a ghost around that old house.

Aunt Margaret told me that when Marcus came up the quarter now, all he and Louise talked about was getting away. Sitting at the table eating supper, or laying across the bed, that was all they talked about. They didn't shut the door any more unless they wanted to bounce, Aunt Margaret said. If all they wanted to do was talk, then they would leave it wide open. They didn't care if she heard what they had to talk about or not. Aunt Margaret said sometimes she would hear Louise crying in the room. Before Marcus came there she had never heard Louise cry in the house once. If she got mad about something, she just clamped her mouth and locked herself up in the room. She wouldn't open the door for Tite, Aunt Margaret or Bonbon. But she didn't do that any more; she cried now when she couldn't have her way.

"Shhh, shhh, we'll do it," Marcus would say to her.

"He won't set the trial," Louise would say. "What's keeping him from setting the trial? He can set it anytime he want."

"Just give him time, honey," Marcus would say to her. "He trying to make me sweat. Now, you got faith in me, don't you?"

"Yes," she would say.

"And that's all that count," Marcus would say.

Then it would be quiet in the room. After a while one of them would get up and latch the door. Now they only latched the door for one reason—bouncing, Aunt Margaret said.

During the day, Louise sat on the gallery or walked around in the yard. If Marshall went by the house in the car, she watched the car until it was out of sight. When she thought it was time for Marshall to come back, she went to the fence so Marshall could see her. She wanted him to see how bad she wanted to get away. Marshall never paid her any mind. He went by the house like he didn't know anything was going on.

Thursday evening, while Louise was sitting on the gallery, she saw Bonbon and Pauline going by in the truck. That night, when Marcus came to the house, she was worse than ever. She had to get away. She had to get away now.

"Get him to set the trial; get him to set the trial," she said. "Don't let him keep us here. Get him to set the trial."

Aunt Margaret sat on the gallery listening to them. Tite had gone to bed, and the door to Louise's bedroom was wide open. Aunt Margaret could hear her crying and Marcus trying to make her stop. But the more he whispered to her, the worse she got. Aunt Margaret felt tears running down her own face, and she raised her hand to wipe them away.

"Don't think I'm crying for y'all," Aunt Margaret thought. "Y'all dead already. I'm crying for the ones go'n have to suffer when y'all gone."

# 47

Marcus went up the quarter with me Friday evening. After he had opened and shut the gate for me, I saw him walking across the yard toward the house. Bishop was coming down the back stairs with the basket on his arm, but when he saw Marcus, he moved back inside and latched the screen door. He didn't take the basket off his arm—he forgot it was there; he said his heart was jumping too much to think of something small as a basket then. "Boy, please don't come here," he was saying to himself. "Please, please don't come here." He heard the gate slam, he heard Marcus coming up the back stairs, then he heard him knocking on the door. And all he could say was, "Boy, please don't come here; please, please don't come here." Marcus knocked again—louder this time. Then he pulled on the door. When he saw the door was latched, he started shaking it by the handle. Bishop said he had backed all the way to the wall, backing the way you back from a man with a gun in his hand. He said he wanted to edge over to the corner and hide, but he was afraid Marcus might hear him moving and know he was in there. He said he had a hard time keeping the basket from falling on the floor; he managed to hold on to it by drawing up his arm.

Marcus shook the door, then he stopped to listen. When nobody showed up, he started shaking the door with all his might. Bishop said it was clear Marcus wasn't leaving from there until somebody came to the door and talked to him.

Then all of a sudden everything got quiet. It was so quiet, Bishop could hear his heart thumping. He shut his eyes and mumbled a prayer to himself. When he opened his eyes, he saw Marshall standing there looking at him. Marshall looked at him with so much hatred, Bishop started backing away from Marshall just like he had backed away from Marcus. Marshall stared at him to make him leave the kitchen. He wouldn't go; he watched Marshall and backed along the wall. Marshall kept on staring at him to make him leave, but still he wouldn't go.

"Get out," Marshall finally told him.

"No sir," he said.

"Get out of here," Marshall told him again.

"No sir," he said. Then he started babbling off at the mouth. "Your people say I can stay here. Your people liked me. They say long as I was a good boy I could stay here. They say if I looked after y'all and I was a good boy, this house was my home till I died. They say that room there 'side that dining room—"

"Didn't I tell you to get out," Marshall said, coming on him.

Bishop slumped to the floor. Marshall grabbed him in the collar and raised him halfway up, then slammed him back down. Bishop hid his face behind the basket that still hung on his arm. Marshall stared down at him a moment before going to the door.

"What do you want?" he said.

"The trial," Marcus said.

It was quiet. Bishop did not raise his head from behind the basket, but he could almost picture the way Marshall looked at Marcus now. He could picture the tightness in Marshall's body and he could picture the way his fist was clenched. He could picture Marshall's cold blue eyes staring at Marcus through the screen door. Bishop wouldn't have been surprised if he had heard a gunshot. But on second thought he knew he wouldn't hear a gunshot; because earlier that day he had heard Marshall talking on the telephone about a trial.

"Be up here Monday at ten o'clock," he heard Marshall saying.

"When can I have the car?" Marcus asked.

It was quiet again. Bishop's face was pressed against the basket. But he didn't have to raise his head to know how Marshall was looking at Marcus. He didn't have to see Marshall's face to know Marshall wanted to kill Marcus where he stood.

"The car'll be there at seven o'clock," Marshall said.

"Where?" Marcus asked.

"By the shop," Marshall said.

"Where Bonbon go'n be?" Marcus asked.

"Mr. Bonbon won't be here," Marshall said.

"You sure now?" Marcus said.

It was quiet again. Bishop wouldn't dare raise his head. Any little unnecessary noise could have made Marshall kill Marcus on those steps.

"Money?" Marcus said. "That little child is sick; we'll need little something to get started with after we get up there."

"The dash drawer," Marshall said.

"The dash draw'?" Marcus asked.

It was quiet a moment, then Marshall repeated what he had said. Marcus told him good night and left.

Marshall didn't move from the door for a long time. Bishop thought he might still hear a gunshot. But after the gate had slammed in the yard, he knew he wouldn't hear any shooting tonight. He felt Marshall looking at him now. His face was pressed against the basket and he was mumbling a prayer to himself. But he wasn't praying for his own safety; he was praying for Marshall and he was praying for the house. He was asking the old people who had died to forgive him for letting them down.

# 48

The next morning, when Aunt Margaret went up the quarter, she found Louise packing her things to leave. Marcus had stopped by there after he left Marshall the night before, and he had told her about the trial and the car. Soon as Bonbon left that morning, Louise started getting ready. When Aunt Margaret got there, she told Aunt Margaret what she wanted her to do. Aunt Margaret told her she knew what she was supposed to do when she came to that house on Saturdays, and she wasn't doing anything this Saturday that she hadn't been doing all the others.

"And we just might not send for you, too," Louise said.

"Yes'm, y'all do that," Aunt Margaret said. "Y'all do exactly that. 'Cause it might be a little inconvenient for me to leave my church and friends—not counting Octave. Y'all do that, Miss Louise; don't send for me."

"Oh, Margaret," Louise said. "You ought to be happy for me. Here, give me your hand. Feel that."

Aunt Margaret jerked her hand back before Louise could lay it on her breast.

"Margaret, me and Judy got to look like niggers," Louise said.

Aunt Margaret acted like she hadn't heard her.

"Where is that child?" she asked.

"At the table."

They were standing in the front room. Now they went back in the kitchen. Tite was sitting at the table eating cush-cush and milk out of a little white pan. She was eating the food with a tablespoon, and she had wasted so much on her dress, she was wet to the skin.

"Master—just look at that," Aunt Margaret said.

"Judy can eat better than that," Louise said.

"Can she?" Aunt Margaret said.

She snatched a dishtowel from a nail against the wall and wiped Tite's face and her dress. Then she sat down at the table to feed Tite the right way.

"Soot good?" Louise said.

Aunt Margaret looked at Louise. She didn't know what Louise was talking about.

"Soot good?" she said. "Now who that suppose to be?"

Louise laughed. "Soot good ain't nobody, Margaret. Soot come out the chimley. Is it good to put on your face?"

"Miss Louise, y'all ain't going nowhere," Aunt Margaret said. She had started to put a spoonful of cush-cush and milk in Tite's mouth, but she stopped to look at Louise. Tite kept her mouth open a second, then she closed it.

"I told you already, Margaret, the trial is Monday," Louise said. "He's going to be innocent. We'll get the car Monday night and leave. Didn't I tell you all that when you walked in the door?"

"Miss Louise, y'all ain't going nowhere," Aunt Margaret said again. She still hadn't put the spoon in Tite's mouth—just holding it there, level-full of cush-cush and milk.

"You don't want us to go, Margaret, do you?" Louise said. She had changed from being happy; she was mad and suspicious of Aunt Margaret, now. "He was right," she said.

239

"You and your kind don't want us to go. It's the end for you and your kind if we get away."

"Miss Louise, I don't know what you talking 'bout," Aunt Margaret said, still holding the food away from Tite.

"I know what I'm talking 'bout," Louise said. "It's all right for Sidney and that—that Pauline down there. But it's not all right for me and Marcus. Well, I say we go, and we will go."

"I just hope this child wasn't in it," Aunt Margaret said, feeding Tite again.

"Well, she is in it," Louise said. "And I don't want you putting any foolishness in her head, either."

"Like what, Miss Louise?"

"You know like what," Louise said. "You in it, too, remember."

She went out of the kitchen. Tite looked over her shoulder at Louise, then she looked at Aunt Margaret. Tite didn't know what was going on, but she knew Aunt Margaret didn't like it. Aunt Margaret said Tite looked at her so sadly, she wanted to squeeze Tite to her bosom.

Louise came back a few minutes later with a little green powder box and a polka-dotted kerchief. She sat across the table from Aunt Margaret and opened the box. Aunt Margaret saw a powder muff inside the box. The top of the powder muff was pink, but as Louise started dipping it in the box, Aunt Margaret saw the bottom part of the muff was black.

"That's soot in that box?" she said.

"That's soot," Louise said. "Come, Judy."

"You know that stuff go'n itch that child?" Aunt Margaret said.

"I'm warning you, don't put foolishness in her head," Louise said. "Come, Judy."

Aunt Margaret wiped Tite's face with the dishtowel, and Tite went to Louise. Louise started patting Tite's face with the powder muff. Aunt Margaret wasn't looking at Tite; she was looking at Louise. She said Louise's face was set the way a woman's face is set when she's cleaning out her child's ear. But Louise didn't look like a woman, she looked like a child playing with a doll.

"Turn the other way," Louise said.

Tite did what she said. Aunt Margaret was still watching Louise, not Tite. Louise dipped the muff inside the box and patted Tite under the chin and around the neck. Then Aunt Margaret, watching Louise all the time, could tell Louise was rubbing the soot into Tite's skin. When she was through, she put the powder muff inside the box, and she tied the kerchief around Tite's head.

"Well?" she said to Aunt Margaret.

Aunt Margaret and Tite looked at each other at the same time. Aunt Margaret felt like somebody had hit her in the chest with his fist. She said Tite looked more like a little nigger than Jobbo's little girl Edna ever did.

"That child still white," she said.

"Where?" Louise said. "You can't see her hair. "I'll put gloves on her hands."

"She still white," Aunt Margaret said.

"Nobody can tell at night."

"And the day?"

"We sleep in the day."

"Sleep where?"

"They have rooms for people."

"A black man, a white woman and a white child leaving the South?"

"We'll sleep," Louise said. "They have good people some-where."

241

"Yes, you'll sleep," Aunt Margaret said. "Y'all go'n sleep."

"Shut up," Louise said. "Shut up. If you can't help me, just shut up."

Tite started crying. Aunt Margaret reached out her hands, and Tite went to her. The water started running down Tite's face, leaving a white trail from her eyes to her mouth. Aunt Margaret picked Tite up and held her in her lap.

"You can wash that off her face when you get up from there," Louise said. "I'll try it one more time before we leave. If it worry her, I'll try something else."

"Y'all ain't going nowhere, Miss Louise," Aunt Margaret said.

Louise had started in the other room, but now she stopped by Aunt Margaret's chair. Aunt Margaret looked up at her standing there with her hand raised. Louise was so mad she had turned red in the face.

"Go on and hit me, Miss Louise," Aunt Margaret said. "Go on and hit me if that make you feel better."

"Margaret, just shut up," Louise said, trembling and crying. "Just shut up. Just shut up, Margaret."

She went out of the room crying. Tite was crying, too. Aunt Margaret rocked Tite in her arms, saying, "Shhh, shhh, shhh."

When Louise first went in her bedroom she laid down on the bed and cried. But after a while she got up and sat before the dresser. Aunt Margaret had started cleaning up the house, and going back and forth by the door, she could see Louise sitting before the looking glass powdering her face.

Aunt Margaret was on the back gallery washing clothes when she heard Louise coming through the house.

"How do I look, Margaret?" Louise said.

Aunt Margaret was rubbing one of Tite's dresses on the washboard. She said she rubbed the dress couple more times before she turned and look at Louise in the door. She said you couldn't tell Louise wasn't colored. She had blacked up her face just the right amount. She had put on a hat with a veil. You couldn't see her yellow hair at all, and you had to raise the veil to see her eyes or her mouth.

"You can pass," Aunt Margaret said.

Louise smiled. "Just like a child," Aunt Margaret thought. "Just lik : a five-year-old child playing out there in the yard."

"Oh, Margaret," Louise said. "Why don't you understand?"

"I think I understand too much already," Aunt Margaret said.

"I mean us."

"I understand y'all, Miss Louise," Aunt Margaret said, and went back to washing.

Louise came closer and put her hand on Aunt Margaret's shoulder.

"Margaret, I wasn't going to hit you in the kitchen," she said.

Aunt Margaret rubbed Tite's dress on the washboard and didn't answer.

"You forgive me, Margaret?"

"Yes'm, I forgive you," Aunt Margaret said.

"Oh, Margaret," Louise said. "We just want to be happy. That's all. That's all, Margaret."

Aunt Margaret turned to look at her. She didn't straighten up, she didn't even take her hands off the washboard.

"Some people can't be happy together, Miss Louise." she said. "It's not made for them to be happy."

"We can," Louise said. "I'm always happy with Marcus."

"It's wrong, Miss Louise," Aunt Margaret said. She said she was talking to her the same way you talk to a child. Louise couldn't understand anything else.

243

"It's not wrong round Yankees," Louise said. "Yankees don't care."

Aunt Margaret said she straightened up now to look at her better.

"Y'all ain't round Yankees, Miss Louise," she said.

"We'll get round them," Louise said. "We won't mix with them, but we'll live there. Judy'll have to go to school with the little Yankees, but I'll tell her not to get too close."

Aunt Margaret said she just stood there looking at Louise's black face through the veil. Even talking to Louise the way you talk to a child wasn't doing any good.

"You not mad at me, Margaret?"

"No, I'm not mad," Aunt Margaret said.

"Oh, Margaret," Louise said, and kissed her on the jaw through the veil. "Margaret, we won't send for you—I was just playing; but I'll write to you, and I'll send you a present. And if you ever want to come there, we'll send you something on your ticket. 'Cause he likes you, too, Margaret. He's always telling me how much he likes you. Just last night he was saying, 'I like that maid you got there.' I said, 'Who? Margaret?' He said, 'Uh-huh, her; I like her.' See?"

"Yes'm, I see," Aunt Margaret said.

Louise smiled.

"Now, you go'n help me?"

Aunt Margaret nodded. "Yes'm, I'll help."

"We have couple more days, but we might 's well start now," Louise said. "After you get through washing, we'll figure out what we need from the store. We'll have to buy something to make sandwiches with. Don't worry 'bout the money. I got little bit saved up. Didn't know I had saved, did you?"

"No'm."

"I got little saved up."

"Don't you think we ought to wait till Monday to make the sandwiches?" Aunt Margaret said.

"Monday? Why?"

"This hot weather, they might spoil."

"Oh, yes, yes, you're right, Margaret. Margaret, you're always so right. Well, what we can do today is wash clothes."

"I'm doing that now, Miss Louise."

"And iron and sew on buttons," Louise said. "We might need a little patching here and there. Oh, my heart is singing, Margaret, I want to fly away."

She held out her arms and started dancing. Aunt Margaret was looking at her all the time, and she soon quit. She grinned at Aunt Margaret—a long, slow, shame-face grin—then she went back inside.

For the rest of that day and all day Monday, Aunt Margaret was helping Louise get ready to leave. But she knew that Louise and Marcus weren't going anywhere.

# 49

Marcus started getting his things together that Sunday a little after twelve. When I came to the door he was sitting on the gallery polishing his shoes. He had six or seven pairs. He had brown and white shoes, black and white shoes, ox-blood shoes; he had plain brown shoes, plain black shoes; he had a pair of yellow, pointed-toed shoes, and he had a pair of gray cloth shoes. He had a bottle of polish and a can of polish for all but the gray shoes. He had two shoe brushes and a couple of shoeshine rags laying on the steps. When I came to the door, he was polishing the oxblood shoes.

"How's it going?" I said.

"Trying to get things together," he said.

He didn't have on a shirt or an undershirt—he wore a pair of brown pants. He had been to the barber the day before; I could see the neat razor line on the back of his neck. Hanging on the clothesline over his head was a bunch of shirts, pants and suits. The shirts were all colors—blue, pink, white, green. He had about a half dozen suits and sports jackets there, too. He had even brought out his suitcases. He had them opened, airing out against the wall.

Marcus called to a little boy going by the gate. The boy came in the yard—no shirt, no shoes, just a pair of overalls that had been torn off at the knees. His face and his body was shining with sweat. His hair looked like grains of black pepper on his head.

"Yes sir?" he said to Marcus.

"Want make a dime?" Marcus said.

"Yes sir."

"Go in the house and get that money off the bed. Then go down to Josie and tell her send me two chicken dinners and some beer. Four bottles of beer. You can remember all that?"

"Yes sir."

"Say it."

The little boy said it.

"All right, get the money and go on," Marcus said.

The little boy ran inside to get the money, then he ran out of the yard and down the quarter. He was spanking his behind the way you spank a horse to make him run faster.

"Want have dinner with me?" Marcus said over his shoulder.

"Don't mind at all."

I went over where he was and sat on the end of the gallery, looking at him.

"Fixing things up," he said.

"Yeah, I see."

He spit on the tip of the oxblood shoe and brushed it down. Then he put the shoe between his knees and started rubbing it with the shoe rag. He rubbed it hard and fast, popping the rag a couple times. When he was through, the gloss on the tip hurt your eyes.

"Pretty good, huh?" he said.

"Yeah," I said.

"Used to do little that for a living," he said.

"Did you?"

"Yeah, long time ago."

247

After he finished with the oxblood shoes, he got the brown ones.

"This time tomorrow, guess that trial be over," he said, thoughtfully. "This time Tuesday I'll be somewhere in Texas."

"California, huh?"

"Yeah, I figure that's the best place for us to go," he said. "They say they got a lot of them army and navy plants out there. Should be able to get some kind of work."

I looked at him, but I didn't say anything. I could feel that tightness in me again. It had been coming and going ever since Marshall first showed up in the field. It was in me Friday evening when Marcus went to that house. I waited for him in the road and asked him what had happened. He told me everything was set. But when I came up to the yard the next day, Bishop came up to me shaking his head. He looked sadder and sicker than I had ever seen him, and he just stood there shaking his head. He didn't say a word, he didn't even try to open his mouth, he just shook his head like doomsday had finally got here. When I saw Marcus again that evening I told him about it, but I could have saved my breath for all the good it did.

Now, Marcus looked up from the shoe he was working on and grinned at me. It was a little knowing grin, like he knew what I had been thinking about all the time.

"Still don't think it's go'n work, huh?" he said.

"Aunt Margaret and Bishop don't think so," I said.

"I don't pay too much 'tention to old people talk," Marcus said.

"That's not a good thing to say, Marcus; not at a time like this."

"Jim, stop being old-fashion," he said. "Where would people be if they didn't take a chance? You know where? Right here. Right here in this quarter the rest of they life."

The little boy came back with the food and the beer.

"Go in my kitchen and get that opener off the table," I told him.

He ran in and ran back out. After handing me the opener, he ran out of the yard. He was the running-est little boy I had ever seen.

We sat there eating. I was hungry because I hadn't ate a thing since last night. I had done some gambling at Josie's place until about four this morning, and I had left there, half broke, without eating anything. I hadn't ate anything when I got up, so right now I was half starved. Marcus was pretty hungry, too. He was tearing into that chicken like he hadn't seen food in days.

The second bell rang for church. I saw people going by the gate. It was hot, and all the women and girls had on light-color dresses. Most of them had straw or pasteboard fans. The men used their pocket handkerchiefs to fan with. The smaller children didn't have anything, and they didn't mind the heat half as much as the older people did. Most of them waved or spoke to me as they went by. They didn't say anything to Marcus; they just looked at his clothes hanging on the line.

"I used to belong to church," Marcus said.

"Yes?" I said.

He could see I wanted him to talk, so he wouldn't say anything else for a while.

"I was baptised when I was about twelve," he said. "Was a good little Christian, too. Used to go to church all the time— me and my mama. People used to say I was go'n be a preacher. I used to read the Bible in the church sometime.

249

Then my mama died. My daddy put me with my nan-nan and he took off somewhere. After he left, I had to get a job to help support myself. I got a job on a parking lot. They had another nigger working there they called Big Red. I wasn't no more than fifteen then, so Big Red showed me the ropes. He charged me a dollar a day for showing me the ropes. I didn't think that was fair and I went to the boss and told him. He told me not to give Big Red a damn thing. I told Big Red what he said. I didn't say the word damn, because I was a Christian and damn was a bad word. I just told Big Red the boss said I didn't have to give him anything.

" 'So you went to the white man, huh?' Big Red said. 'For that you go'n give me two dollars a day. Now, go tell the white man that.'

"I went and told the white man Big Red said I had to give him two dollars a day. He said I didn't have to give Big Red a damn thing. I asked him to tell Big Red that because Big Red wouldn't believe me. He told me he was a little busy then, but for me to go out there and tell Big Red what he said. I didn't tell Big Red anything because now I saw what was going on. Big Red was his number one nigger, and he didn't care what Big Red did.

"So I went to Jesus on my knees. Every night before I went to bed I asked Jesus to go with Big Red. I figured if He blessed Big Red, Big Red would leave me 'lone. Big Red might even take pity on me, seeing I was a little boy, and even give me some money. But that was the farthest thing from Big Red's mind. Every day just 'fore I knocked off, he came to me and asked me for his two dollars. If I told him I hadn't made that much tip, he jugged his hand in my pocket and took everything. I wanted to quit the job, but my nan-nan told me not to. She said the white man would put a bad mark behind my name and it would be hard for me to get another job anywhere else in Baton Rouge. So I stayed there. I stayed there, and every night I prayed. I prayed so much, I even mentioned Big Red's name in church. But instead of me saying, 'Jesus, go with Big Red,' I said, 'Jesus, please make Big Red stop taking my money.' When I said that, the church cracked up. Everybody started laughing. Even the preacher on the pulpit. Everybody laughing and coughing and wiping they eyes. Because, you see, Jesus didn't do things like that. Jesus healed the sick and raised the dead, but He didn't stop people from taking your money. That wasn't a miracle—not even a little miracle.

"The next day when I went to work, Big Red said, 'I hear you been talking 'bout me to a Jew now. That go'n cost you another dollar.'

"That night he came to collect his three dollars. I had just bought a big bottle of pop.

" 'All right, pay off,' he said. 'Don't try to hold back, I'll just go in your pocket.'

"I paid him off, all right. I splintered that bottle on his head.

"But 'fore I could move, the law was there hauling me off to jail. They put me in a cell with about six other niggers. They called one of them Cadillac. Soon as I got in there, Cadillac said, 'You brought my cigarettes?'

" 'No,' I said.

" 'You shouldn't come to a man house and don't bring his cigarettes,' he said, and rammed his fist in my stomach. I went down. He picked me up and hit me again. He beat me so bad I couldn't even go to my bunk. Two other niggers had to take me there. The next morning the jailer looked at me all bruised, but he didn't say a thing. He even gived

Cadillac more food than he gived the rest of us. Cadillac was his nigger just like Big Red was the other white man's nigger.

"When my nan-nan came to see me, I told her to bring me some cigarettes next time. She bought the cigarettes 'fore she left the jail, and I gived them to Cadillac. That went on every time she came. She gived me the cigarettes and I gived them to Cadillac. When Cadillac got out, somebody else came in. They called him Horse Trader and he said he was Cadillac cousin. He told me Cadillac told him to collect the cigarettes I owed him. So when my nan-nan came now, I gived the cigarettes to Horse Trader. I wasn't the only one Cadillac and Horse Trader did this to; they did it to everybody they could. Horse Trader even made people suck him off. Not me, some other cats. If he had ever tried that on me, I woulda killed him while he slept. But he tried that on other people. If the jailer caught anybody sucking anybody off, he took the person who was doing the sucking to another room and beat the hell out of him and brought him right back. And Horse Trader would make him suck him off again. Horse Trader had a favorite one, a little yellow cat called Chinaman. Horse Trader used to make Chinaman hit it every night. Every time Chinaman got through, he puked and prayed to Jesus. Every night he had to eat, then he puked and prayed. I could have told him praying wasn't going to do any good, but I thought I better keep out of this shit. One day they took Chinaman off to Jackson to the crazy house.

"When Horse Trader got out of jail, another one came in. I forgot his name—Boxcar, or something—and he said he was Horse Trader half-brother. So I gived the cigarettes to Boxcar. Then one day I told myself I ain't giving these fuckers nothing no more even if they killed me. If I had to go through life like that, life wasn't worth it. So I told my nan-nan to stop bringing cigarettes. She wouldn't stop. So everytime she brought them, I ripped open the pack and dumped them in the toilet. Boxcar beat me every time I did that, but I didn't care no more.

"When they let me out of jail, I promised myself I was go'n look out only for myself; and I wasn't go'n expect no more from life than what I could do for myself. And nobody in this world need to expect no more from me than that."

"You can't make it like that, Marcus," I said. "They got the world fixed where you have to work with other people."

"Not me," he said.

"Yes, you, Marcus," I said. "Yes, you. You, me and everybody else."

"Not me," he said. " 'Cause I already know 'em. No matter what they say, it don't add up to nothing but a big pile of shit. You do what you can do for yourself, and that's all."

Up the quarter, the people were singing and praying in the church. I looked at Marcus, and I felt empty inside. I felt empty because he could not believe in God or friendship; I felt empty because I doubted if I believed in anything, either.

# 50

The next morning, when I came to the yard, Bonbon was there already. He told me Marcus wasn't going in the field with me that morning, he had to go for his trial. He said Marcus would be out there that evening, though, so it wasn't any need for me to get anybody in his place. At ten o'clock, he took Marcus to Bayonne in the truck. Marcus wore his black suit, his white shirt and his black and white shoes. The trial was at ten thirty. At eleven thirty the trial was over, and at ten minutes to twelve Bonbon had Marcus in the quarter again. When he stopped before the gate, he told Marcus to go in and change clothes because the honeymoon was over.

Charlie Jordan lived right across the road from us. Charlie was sitting out on his gallery with his right foot in a pan of Epsom salt water. Charlie said he could see how Bonbon and Marcus were talking to each other, then glaring at each other, but he didn't know what it was all about. Marcus walked away from the truck. Bonbon watched him a few seconds, then he swung the truck around and went speeding back up the quarter. Charlie said the dust in the road was flying so much you couldn't see the house next to yours. Bonbon went up to the big house and knocked on the screen door, but he jerked the door open before anybody could answer.

"Where is the old man?" he said to Bishop.

Bishop went to get Marshall. When they came back in the kitchen, Pauline was there, too. She stood by the stove, pretending to be busy.

"Yes?" Marshall said.

"What's with that boy down there?" Bonbon said.

"What boy?" Marshall said.

"The one I take to Bayonne."

"Did he say anything to you?"

"He say something to me, all right," Bonbon said. "He's innocent and don't have to go back in that field."

"He is innocent," Marshall said. "I just got a call from Bayonne."

"Innocent?" Bonbon said.

"Yes," Marshall said. "Didn't you go to the trial?"

"I got other things to do," Bonbon said. "When they start deciding these things at trial?"

"I thought they always did," Marshall said.

"Yes?" Bonbon said.

"Yes," Marshall said. "But maybe I've been wrong all these years."

Now they just looked at each other. Bonbon knew Marshall was lying. He knew Marshall had it fixed from the start. Marshall knew Bonbon knew this. Bonbon turned to leave, and Marshall stopped him again. Bonbon didn't turn around this time, he looked over his shoulder at Marshall.

"I want you to take me somewhere this evening," Marshall said. "To see that bull there of Jacques. Be here at six o'clock."

Bonbon went out. Marshall went back up the hall. Bishop and Pauline stood in the kitchen looking at each other. Pauline said, "Innocent? Innocent? Did he say he was innocent?" Bishop didn't answer her. Bishop didn't like Pauline at all, but this was not the reason he didn't answer her now. He didn't answer her because he felt too weak to answer her. He felt too weak to be standing there, too. He should have been laying down with a cold towel on his forehead.

Pauline heard the tractor coming up the quarter and she

came out in the yard to meet me. She was at the crib when I drove up there. That was the first time since I had been on that plantation when I wasn't glad to see Pauline. I parked the tractor in front of the crib and jumped down to see what she wanted.

"What's going on, Jim," she asked me.

"What's the matter?" I said.

"Marcus innocent."

"He is?" I said.

"You mean he don't pay for killing that boy?" she asked.

"I guess not—if he's innocent," I said.

"What's going on, Jim?" she said, looking straight at me. "What's going on round here?"

"I don't know," I said.

"Yes, you do," she said. "What's going on round here, Jim?"

"Keep out of this, Pauline," I said.

"Keep out of what?" she said.

"Just keep out of everything," I said, turning away from her.

She grabbed me by the arm.

"What's going on, Jim? What's going on round here?"

She was squeezing my arm. Any other time I would have liked this. Right now I was just scared.

"Keep out of this, please, Pauline," I said. "Keep out of this."

"What's going on, Jim?"

"Even if you knew, you couldn't do a thing about it, Pauline," I said.

"Is it something to do with Sidney?"

"Bonbon's wife," I said.

"What is it, Jim?"

"You keep your mouth shut, now."

"What is it?"

"Marcus and Louise running away from here tonight."

Pauline covered her mouth with her hand. I could see how her eyes were thinking. I could see how she couldn't believe this and how, after a while, she did believe it. Then I could see how she was asking herself, "Why? Why? Why?"—then I could see her answering her own question. Her hand came slowly from her mouth.

"I see," she said. "I see. And me?"

"You'll have to get away from here, too," I said.

"Go where? Do what?"

"Don't you have people?"

The way she looked at me, I could see she didn't want to go round her people. And maybe, after the way she had been living with Bonbon, her people didn't want her there, either.

"Don't stay up here tonight, Pauline," I said. "There might be trouble."

She didn't answer me; she didn't care any more.

"You heard me?" I said to her.

She didn't answer. She looked down at the ground. She didn't care about anything any more.

"Go back inside, Pauline. You don't have anything on your head," I said.

She looked up at me now. I could see she didn't care about anything. She turned from me and went back toward the house.

When I came out in the road, I could see the truck parked in front of Bonbon's house. As I came closer, I saw Bonbon coming out in the road to wave me down. I stopped the tractor and Bonbon came closer to talk over the noise the tractor was making. I jumped down to hear him better.

"Take Jonas with you," he said.

"Something the matter?"

"That boy went free."

"Free?" I said.

"Free," he said. "They had it rigged from the start. The boy he kill don't mean a thing."

"Maybe the boy was wrong," I said.

"No, they had it rigged," Bonbon said. "Even if the boy was wrong, you just don't go free, Geam. They had it rigged. There, they got me working that boy out there and they laughing at me behind my back. They make me the fool."

"They haven't started with you yet," I thought. "Wait until tomorrow this time."

"Take Jonas," he said.

"You'll be out later?"

"No, I don't think so. Little work I got to 'tend to down the river. Got to take the old man somewhere this evening."

I nodded.

"Listen, Geam," he said. "Y'all take it easy out there. Corn getting thinner and we ought to finish by the weekend anyhow. How far you from that ditch now?"

"I don't know. Fifteen, eighteen rows."

"Go to the ditch and knock off," he said.

"Right."

I started to get back on the tractor. He stopped me again.

"Geam?" he said. "What you think 'bout that? You think he ought to go free?"

"What can I say? That's the way they work it."

"Yeah, you right," Bonbon said. "Me and you—what we is? We little people, Geam. They make us do what they want us to do, and they don't tell us nothing. We don't have nothing to say 'bout it, do we, Geam?"

"Not very much," I said.

"Take Jonas," he said.

I got back on the tractor and drove away. When I looked over my shoulder I saw him going back in the yard. He walked with his head down. He was still thinking about what they had done to him.

# 51

Marcus was at the house when I got there. He was laying down on the bed in his room. He had packed everything but the clothes he was going to wear that night. His brown pants and blue silk shirt were hanging on a coat hanger against the wall. His gray shoes were on the floor by the window. Marcus was laying on the bed in nothing but his shorts.

"Well, it's over," he said, when I came in the room.

"Heard about it."

"Yeah, it's over," he said, smiling.

"Want a beer?" I asked him.

"I put a few more bottles in there," he said. "Went over to Josie and got a few more."

"You and Josie speaking now?"

"Yeah, we made up. I told her I was checking out of here this evening. Told her with who and she started laughing."

"You told her you and Louise were leaving together?"

"Yeah. She didn't believe me at first. She believe me now, though."

"You take a big chance, Marcus."

"Well, who go'n tell?" he said.

He followed me around the other side. He still didn't have on a thing but his shorts.

"Hungry?" I asked him.

"No," he said. "Might eat later. I warmed it up for you."

"Thanks," I said.

I could smell the food soon as I walked in the kitchen. I had cooked up some beef meat the night before, and I had seasoned it down with onion and bell pepper. I had cooked up a pot of rice to go with it. After washing my face and hands, I dished up my dinner and sat down at the table. Marcus had already opened up two bottles of beer.

"Yeah, this is it," he said again.

"Here's to you," I said, raising my bottle.

He raised his bottle, too. I ate and looked at him. I could still feel that tightness in me. It was in me all morning. No matter what I thought, no matter what I said, it wouldn't leave.

"Listen, Marcus," I said. "You free, huh?"

"Yeah. Free."

"Then why don't you take off now?"

"Take off?"

"Yeah. Now."

"How 'bout her?"

"That's another man's wife, Marcus," I said. "And she's a white woman."

"So?" he said.

"Listen, Marcus," I said. "Do you really care anything for that woman?"

"Yeah," he said. He didn't say it too strongly, though.

"Do you, Marcus?"

"Yeah," he said, a little stronger. "Yeah, I think I do. Yeah, I do. Maybe I didn't till just now—till you asked me. Now, I know I love her. It wouldn't be the same 'thout her. Yeah, I love her—love that little woman. Ain't claiming she much to look at—nobody in his right mind can honestly say that; but I love her anyhow. 'Cause I know she love me. Ain't never had nobody to love me like that. Warming up food for me and bringing it to the bed. Crying like that over me . . ."

"Nothing can change your mind, now?"

"Nothing," he said.

"Before, all you wanted was to get away from here."

"Now, I want bo' of us to get 'way from here," he said. "She much slave here as I was."

"Can't you leave and send for her? I mean, leave right now and send for her?"

"How can she ever get out of here by herself?" he said. "She can't even get out of that yard 'fore somebody round here spot her and tell. She told me herself she ain't been out of that yard in over a year. I think that's why I love her—I don't know. I guess y'all didn't know I had that kind of heart, did y'all?"

I didn't answer him, I just looked at him. He was sweating on the nose.

"Six more hours in this quarter, and good-bye," he said. "Good-bye Louisiana, good-bye South."

"I hope you change your mind and take off now," I said. "I don't feel good about all this waiting."

"Can't do it," he said. He drank some beer. "She need me. She need my arms round her. Told me that herself. She said, 'Marky-poo—' that's what she call me when we by usself. She said, 'Marky-poo, 'thout you I'll go crazy.' That's what she told me. ' 'Thout you I'll go crazy, Marky-poo. I need your arms round me. I need your arms round me all the time, Marky-poo.' "

He stretched out his arm and looked at it.

"Pretty good arm, huh?" he said.

I nodded. He was the same Marcus. No matter whatever happened, he was still going to be the same Marcus.

"Say she like the color my arms," he said, twisting his arm one way, then the other way.

"Did she?" I said.

"What she said," he said, still looking at his arm. Then

he looked at me. "Sweet little woman just like you see her there," he said. "Can be a little devil at time, though; just like any other woman."

"Well, I guess I said all I can. I hope you'll change your mind, but I guess I can't make you."

"No, no use talking 'bout it," he said.

I finished eating and sat there drinking another beer with him.

"Who taking my place?" he asked.

"Fellow named Jonas," I said.

"Oh, yeah, that slow-walking nigger," he said. "Talk slow, too."

"Yeah, he's pretty slow," I said.

"Well, long as he don't work slow," Marcus said. "Them freaks out there'll kill him." He laughed. "Them two freaks sure didn't like me. Well, they can have it. They b'longs out there, I don't. And you don't, either, Jim."

"Nobody's wife asked for my arms."

"Well, you wouldn't have too much trouble," Marcus said.

I sat there, looking at him. I still didn't feel good about him hanging round here like that. When I got ready to go back in the field, I told him I would come in early enough to see him off. He said he would like that. We shook hands. He squeezed my hand pretty hard. After I had gone out in the road and cranked up the tractor, I looked back at him again. He stood in the door, waving at me.

# 52

Aunt Ca'line said the whole evening was just too quiet. She said usually it was quiet after everybody had gone back in the field, leaving just the old people and the small children in the quarter, but this day was particularly quiet. She said she mentioned the quietness to Pa Bully several times and he nodded his head. Since they knew about the trial and what Marcus was supposed to do later (Josie had already spread the news), she and Pa Bully could do no more than just look at each other. Pa Bully tried to hide his fear just like she tried to pretend she was braver than what she was; but after you've been living with another person so long, there's not too much he doesn't already know about you. The sun was at the back of the house, so they sat out on the front gallery. The housework she had to do ("little cleaning, little cooking") she had done since that morning, so now all she had to do was sit out on the gallery with her husband. When it got cooler, maybe she would go out in her garden.

" 'Member the time they lynched Coon boy," Pa Bully said. He was going to say more, but Aunt Ca'line looked at him to make him stop. As she said later, she remembered the day herself. The air smelt just like it did today, the place was quiet just like it was today, and it was clear and bright and hot just like it was today. So she didn't want to hear about it.

Charlie Jordan said since the sun was on his front gallery, he sat in a chair just inside the front door. Every time the sun moved a little closer toward him, he moved a little farther inside the room. But each time he moved his chair, he made sure he kept it so he could look at Marcus on the other side of the road. He said the foot he had stuck that nail in this morning was still hurting him, and he had tied a piece of salt meat on the foot to draw the soreness out. If it wasn't for this, he would have been in the cotton field with his children. But since he couldn't go out there, then he just sat in his room with his chair facing the door, watching Marcus. Like Pa Bully and Aunt Ca'line, he had already heard about the trial and he had heard what Marcus was supposed to do this evening. He was scared and at the same time he was proud of Marcus. Marcus had got away with something most of the people around there would have been afraid to think about. He saw Marcus come out on the gallery and stand with his hands on his hips. After looking up and down the quarter, he went back in again. Charlie could see him pacing the floor just inside the room. Then a few minutes later he was on the gallery again, this time with a bottle of beer. He was still in his shorts. Charlie said he would stand in one place awhile, then he would start pacing the gallery. Then he would go in my room or his room. Every time he went in my room he came back with a bottle of beer, Charlie said.

Charlie made a pot of coffee and came back to his chair again. Charlie had to walk on the heel of his right foot because he had stuck the nail right smack in the center. He said he didn't know what possessed children to stick nails up in the road when people went barefooted all the time.

Charlie Jordan drank coffee and watched Marcus. Even when Marcus wasn't on the gallery, Charlie still looked over there. Then Marcus would show up again. Charlie said he must have come out there and went back in a dozen times that evening. He was like a lion—back and forth, back and forth, Charlie said.

Around four o'clock, Charlie said, the pain in his foot really hit him. The sweat started pouring off him like rain water. He made it to the bed and laid down. Now he started shaking. He was shaking like he had the chills. But it wasn't chills, he said later. It was just plain fear. It wasn't until then that he realized what could happen to Marcus. He said once his teeth started rattling in his mouth, and he had to bite down on the sheet to keep them still.

Aunt Margaret said by the time Marcus came back from the trial, she and Louise had packed everything. And she was scared every second of this time. Once she got so weak she couldn't tie the string on the food box, and Louise had to help her. After they had packed everything and pushed everything under the bed, Louise powdered her face again. She even looked more colored than she did last Saturday morning. She was getting the feel of it now and she knew exactly how much she needed to put on. And with her hat and veil on, nobody could possibly take her for a white person. She powdered up Tite again, too. With the polka dot kerchief on Tite's head, Tite could have passed for one of Jobbo's little girls, Aunt Margaret said.

When Tite, Bonbon and Louise were sitting at the table at twelve o'clock, Tite said:

"J'n neg, Papa?"

"Kess-koo-sey?" Bonbon said.

"Playing with that mud out there and smeared mud on her face," Louise said. "Now she thinks she's a nigger."

"No neg," Bonbon said to Tite. "No neg."

"No neg?" Tite said, shaking her head.

"No neg," Bonbon said, shaking his head. "No neg."

After Bonbon left the house, Aunt Margaret and Tite sat out on the gallery. Louise was checking the place to see if she had forgot anything. She was taking just food and clothes. And that's why Bonbon hadn't missed anything. He had to look inside the dresser or the armoire to miss her clothes, and he didn't have any reason at all to go in either one.

Around three o'clock, Tite fell asleep in Aunt Margaret's arms, and Aunt Margaret laid her down on a little pallet on the gallery. Then she sat back in her chair and looked down at Tite. The tears started running down her face. She didn't know how hard she was crying until Louise came to the door and put her hand on her shoulder.

At five o'clock, she got ready to leave the house. Tite was up again. Aunt Margaret, Tite and Louise were standing on the gallery. Aunt Margaret picked up Tite and held her close, then she put her back down. She looked at Louise.

"Anything in there you want?" Louise asked.

Aunt Margaret said she wanted to say, "You ain't going nowhere, Miss Louise. I can tell from the weather y'all ain't leaving this place." But she only shook her head.

"Good-bye, Margaret," Louise said.

Aunt Margaret went down the steps. At the gate, she looked back at them again. They still watched her from the gallery. She turned from the gate and went out in the road. The dust was so white and hot it made her eyes burn, she said.

About five thirty, Bonbon went up to the big house. Bishop said Pauline was still there. She could have been gone since three thirty, but she stayed because she knew Bonbon was coming back. When he came in, she asked him if he wanted to eat. He sat down at the table and she fixed him up a big plate of food. Bishop and Bonbon looked at each other once or twice, but they didn't say anything. Neither one of them liked the other one, and both of them knew it. But right now, Bishop didn't feel hate for Bonbon. He felt just plain fear—and he already knew he couldn't do a thing about it. He couldn't run because he didn't know where to go. There wasn't any place for him to go. This house and this yard was the only place he had.

While Bonbon ate his food, Pauline sat across from him drinking coffee. They were quiet most of the time, with Pauline looking across the table at Bonbon. Bishop said she knew what was going to happen and she hoped Bonbon did too, but she knew she couldn't tell him. Bishop was in the dining room most of the time—shining wine glasses that didn't need shining—but a couple times he went back in the kitchen where Pauline and Bonbon were. Pauline was still looking across the table at Bonbon. Bonbon went on eating without paying her any mind.

"I keep thinking 'bout Baton Rouge," she was saying. "It was good there—us in that room—wind blowing the curtain. You remember?"

He ate and didn't say anything.

"I liked it there," she said. "I didn't want ever leave. You don't know how you look, sleeping like that—the wind blowing the curtain. Remember when you woke up and I told you?"

He didn't say anything.

"I want it to be like that again," she said. "I want it to stay like that. Get in a place where we don't ever have to leave. You think it'll ever be like that again?"

He didn't answer her. He wasn't even looking at her. He went on eating.

"Promise me it'll be like that again," she said. "I'll do anything you say, you promise me that."

Bishop didn't know if Bonbon looked at her or not. Bishop went back in the dining room. A minute later, Marshall went by the dining room with a paper bag. Bishop could hear Marshall saying to Bonbon, "Meet you downstairs in a minute. Going in my car." Then Bishop heard the screen door shut. He went to the window—shining a wine glass that didn't need shining—and looked at Marshall walking 'cross the yard toward the field car. Marshall opened the door and got inside. But when he got back out, he didn't have the paper bag with him any more. Bishop shook his head. That was too big for money, he thought.

In the kitchen, Pauline was saying, "Promise me, promise me."

"What's the matter with you?" Bonbon asked her.

"Promise me we spend another day together like that," she said.

"I see you tonight," Bonbon said.

"You promise that?" Pauline said. "You promise that? Promise me."

Bonbon went out. Bishop heard the door slam behind him. After the car had driven across the yard, Bishop left the dining room. He was going to his own room and lay down, but he stopped to look at Pauline. She stood at the screen door, gazing out in the yard. When she realized Bishop was in the kitchen, she turned to look at him. Her face showed so much hatred for him, Bishop had to walk away. He went to his room and laid down on the bed. A few minutes later, he heard Pauline leaving the house.

It was quiet in the house now. Bishop had shut his door and window to make the room dark. Now, he laid on his bed listening and waiting. He didn't know what he was going to hear, but he knew he was going to hear something.

# 53

I should have got back to the quarter no later than six o'clock, but just as we knocked off, the tractor went dead on me. My heart jumped in my throat because I didn't know how long it was going to take me to get the tractor fixed. Freddie and them didn't know either, and since they had already heard about what Marcus was supposed to do, they didn't want to hang around the fields too late and they started out for home. I started to leave with them and come back to fix the tractor later, but I told myself that fixing the tractor was my work just like driving it.

It took me an hour to get the tractor running again. The sun was already down when I finally hit the road. I didn't have any lights on the tractor, but still I drove her fast as she could go. I knew it was getting close to seven o'clock, and I knew Marcus was getting ready to leave. I wanted to be there to say good-bye to him. No matter what a person does, there ought to be somebody on his side at the last moment. And what had Marcus done that was so wrong? Yes, he had killed—yes, yes—but didn't they give him the right to kill? I had been thinking about this in the field all evening and I had said to myself, "Yes, yes; it's not Marcus, it's them. Marcus was just the tool. Like Hotwater was the tool—put there for Marcus to kill. Like Bonbon was the tool—put there to work Marcus. Like Pauline was a tool, like Louise was a tool. . . ." So I didn't blame Marcus any more. Yes, in a way I did, because I still didn't think it was right to kill. And I didn't think it was right to go free after killing. But what could I do against this big thing that said Yes. I couldn't do a thing. Bonbon had said, "We is nothing but little people. They make us do what they want us to do and they don't tell us nothing." So why blame Marcus? Why blame him? No, I didn't blame Marcus any more. I admired Marcus. I admired his great courage. And that's why I wanted to hurry up and get to the front. That's why my heart had jumped in my throat when the tractor went dead on me—I was afraid I wouldn't be able to tell him how much I admired what he was doing. I wanted to tell him how brave I thought he was. He was the bravest man I knew, the bravest man I had ever met. Yes, yes, I wanted to tell him that. And I wanted to tell Louise how I admired her bravery. I wanted to tell them that they were starting something—yes, that's what I would tell them; they were starting something that others would hear about, and understand, and would follow. "You are both very brave and I worship you," I was going to say. And I was going to shake Marcus's hand, and I was going to kiss Louise on the jaw—that's if she let me. And I was going to ask them to let me buy candy for Tite. Yes, I would buy a big bag of candy so she would always remember that there was somebody on her side when she went away.

I didn't slow up at all from the time I left the field until I came in the quarter. Soon as I crossed the railroad tracks, I could see how dark and quiet the quarter was. There wasn't a light on in any house. There wasn't a child playing anywhere. Nobody sat out on the gallery waiting for supper to be done. Not even a speck of smoke came from any of the kitchen chimleys. The whole place was so dark and quiet, it looked like everybody had moved away. But they hadn't moved away, they had locked themselves inside the houses. All of them had heard what Marcus was supposed to do and all of them were afraid. It was the same fear that made me hate Marcus at first. It was fear for myself and all the rest. The fear was still in me, but I didn't blame Marcus for it any more. Because it wasn't Marcus who was doing this; it was the big people.

I drove through the quarter just as fast as I had driven from the field. There wasn't any need to go slow now, because everybody was inside. When I came up to my house, I saw Marcus's door wide open. I stopped the tractor and ran in to see if he was there. His suitcases were gone, so I knew he had left already. I ran back out and got on the tractor. Maybe I would catch him at the other house. I thought I saw the small red light of a car way up the quarter, and I drove the tractor fast as it could go. Then I saw the red light turn out of the quarter, and I thought I had missed Marcus for sure now. I felt a big lump in my throat because I wanted to see him before he got away. Seeing how all the people had locked themselves inside, I felt more proud of Marcus now than I ever did. I wanted to tell Louise how proud I was of her, too.

Then I saw somebody running toward me. It was getting very dark now and I couldn't tell who it was until he was right on the tractor. Then I recognized Sun Brown. He acted like he didn't see the tractor. If I hadn't ducked out of his way, he might have run right into me.

"Sun?" I hollered at him. "Sun? What's the matter? Sun? Sun?"

He kept running. He was running like a man who was very tired. He could hardly move his legs, and still he was running.

I was coming up to Bonbon's house now. I saw a car parked before the gate. As I came closer, I saw it was the '41 Ford Marcus was supposed to leave in. The front door on the driver's side was opened. The rear door on the other side was opened, too. I stopped the tractor and jumped down. I looked in the back of the car and I saw a pasteboard box on the seat. I looked toward the house. The house was dark. But

I thought I saw somebody sitting on the steps. I went up to the gate to get a closer look. Yes, somebody was sitting on the steps. I pulled the gate open and went in the big yard. I thought the dog was going to start barking at me, but he never did. Later, I learned that Louise had locked the dog in the kitchen when Marcus came there to get her and Tite. I went up to the small gate, and I saw it was Bonbon sitting on the steps with Tite in his arms. Laying on the ground to the left of the steps was Marcus. I pulled the gate open and went in the yard. The front of Marcus's clothes was black with blood. I knelt down beside him to brush some dirt from his face, and that's when I noticed Louise crawling from under the house. Louise wore a light-color dress, and her face was black. The little girl's face was black, too, who laid in Bonbon's arms. Louise's right hand was up to her mouth—no, not the hand, the tip of her fingers. She didn't see anybody but Marcus. I'm not sure she saw him either—she just knew where he was. She knelt down 'side me, without seeing me, gazing down at Marcus all the time. Then she brought her right hand slowly from her mouth and touched his face. She touched it lightly, almost not touching it at all. She touched his hair and his ear just as lightly. Then she touched his face like that again.

"You hurt, Marky-poo?" she said softly. "You hurt?"

I started to pull her away from him, but I changed my mind. It wasn't because Bonbon was sitting there—I didn't care about Bonbon. I didn't care if he killed me just like he had killed Marcus. I didn't pull her away from him because this was going to be their last time together.

"You hurt, Marky-poo?" she said again. "You hurt?"

She laid her face against his. She didn't say another word long as I was there; she didn't even cry.

The reason why Sun had been running in the road was because he had seen it all. This is what he saw.

# 54

Sun Brown had gone to Frank Morris's plantation earlier that day. His sister had sent word that her oldest girl was in trouble, and Sun had gone there to see what he could do. He and his sister and the girl sat out on the gallery talking all evening. The girl was in trouble, all right; she had got caught and the boy didn't want to marry her. Around five o'clock, when Sun got ready to leave, they still didn't know what they were going to do about the girl. Sun promised to send a few dollars whenever he could spare it; then he left for home. Hebert's plantation was six or seven miles from Morris's plantation, and Sun had to walk all the way. Around six thirty, he came up to Jacques Guerin's place and he saw Bonbon and Marshall and Jacques and two or three other Cajuns standing along the fence, looking at a Brahma bull in the yard. Sun stopped in the road to look at the bull. He didn't care about the bull, but he didn't feel good passing his boss and his overseer without speaking. They hadn't seen him because all of them had their backs turned toward the road. Marshall pulled out his watch and checked the time and put the watch back in his pocket. Bonbon looked over his shoulder and saw Sun standing out there. Sun raised his hand and waved. Bonbon didn't wave back; he just looked at Sun, wondering why he was out there. Sun wanted to tell Bonbon he had got permission from Mr. Marshall to go visit his sister, but Bonbon was too far away. Sun didn't know what to do, so he grinned and waved again. Marshall and the other Cajuns looked at him, and he waved at Marshall. Like Bonbon, Marshall didn't wave back, either. He pulled out his watch to check the time again. When the bull went across the yard, everybody turned to look at the bull.

Sun started walking. He wasn't thinking about the men who hadn't waved at him, he wasn't thinking about his pregnant niece, he was just thinking about the hardship man had to live with. Sun thought he had as much hardship as any other man—and maybe a little more. When he came up to the plantation store, he remembered that Sarah had told him to buy some rice and a piece of salt meat. He went inside and he noticed that there weren't any Negroes at the store. Old Godeau asked him where everybody was, and he said he didn't know. After paying for the rice and meat, he started for home. As he came in the quarter, he noticed how quiet everything was. He couldn't understand why it was like this and why he felt scared all of a sudden. He started looking for people in the road, but there wasn't a person anywhere. When he came up to Mrs. Laura Mae's house, he hollered in at her. Mrs. Laura Mae didn't answer him. That was strange, because usually Mrs. Laura Mae was sitting on the gallery this time of evening and she loved talking to people. Sun felt more scared now and walked faster. Then he saw a car coming toward him—no, he saw the dust. The dust was flying all over the quarter. In front of the dust was a car, coming up the quarter with no lights on. The car stopped in front of Bonbon's house, and somebody got out and ran in the yard. Sun had come up to the car by the time the other person came back with a package in his arms, and now he saw that the other person was Marcus. Marcus threw the package on the back seat of the car and ran back in the yard. Sun was so dumbfounded he couldn't move. He couldn't understand what was going on, either. Marcus and Louise running away together was the last thing to come in his mind.

Then he looked over his shoulder. He had not heard the

other car, he had not seen any lights—because there weren't any lights; he had felt the other car coming toward him. He wanted to run, but he couldn't run. So he fell in the ditch and crawled in a bunch of weeds where they wouldn't see him.

The car stopped and Bonbon got out. He looked at the car and looked toward the house before he went in the yard. Sun could tell that Bonbon didn't know what was going on, either. After Bonbon had gone in the yard, Marshall got out of his car and went to the field car. Sun could see him searching in the dashdrawer. Then he got out of the car with a paper bag. He took the bag to his own car and drove away. Sun was watching Bonbon now. Bonbon still had not gotten to the gallery—he still didn't know what was going on. He had even stopped on the walk and looked back toward the road so Marshall could tell him what was happening. He didn't start toward the gallery again until Marshall had driven away. Sun looked toward the gallery. Marcus, Louise and Tite were standing there. Marcus was in front with a package in his arms, and Louise was behind him, holding Tite by the hand. Bonbon still didn't know what was going on—Sun could tell by the slow, careful, thinking way he went toward the house. Then as he came in the small yard, Marcus threw the package to the side and jumped on the ground to fight him. Sun said Marcus had all the chance in the world to get away from there, and he couldn't understand why Marcus didn't run. Sun was screaming inside—"Run, boy; run, run, run." But instead, Marcus jumped on the ground to fight. Bonbon moved toward the house quickly now. When he came to the end of the gallery, he stooped over and picked up something by the steps. Sun could tell that it was a scythe-blade, and not a hoe or a shovel, from the way Bonbon swung it at Marcus. Marcus ran to the fence and jerked loose a picket that was used there for a prop. He and Bonbon started fighting. Marcus was blocking the scythe-blade more than he was trying to hit with the picket. Sun could hear the noise that steel made against wood and that wood made against wood. He wanted to run, but he couldn't run. He couldn't even shut his eyes or plug up his ears.

When the fight started, Louise jumped off the gallery and crawled under the house. The little girl started toward the steps, but the sound of blade against wood and wood against wood made her move back. She tried again—she tried several times; but each time she did, it looked like Marcus and Bonbon were fighting right by the steps, and Tite had to go back upon the gallery.

Sun still wanted to run, but he couldn't run. Even when Marshall Hebert went back up the quarter—with the lights on and driving fast—Sun still couldn't get up and run. He couldn't get his eyes off that little girl who was trying to come down those steps.

Then, for a second, everything was too quiet. Then he heard a scream, and he jerked his head to the left. He saw that Marcus had lost the picket and he saw Bonbon raising the blade. He had time to shut his eyes, and even though he couldn't see, he heard when the blade hit. When he was able to look again, he saw Bonbon standing there with the blade in his hand. Bonbon swung the blade far across the yard and went up on the gallery to get his little girl. He sat down on the steps with the little girl in his arms.

Sun still couldn't move. He didn't move until he heard the tractor coming up the quarter. Then he jumped up and started running. He ran all the way home. He didn't tell anybody what he had seen. He wouldn't tell anybody what he had seen for a whole week. He wouldn't even come out of his house. The only person he let come to him was his smallest daughter who was too young to talk and ask questions.

# 55

There wasn't a trial, there was a hearing. Bonbon got off with justifiable homicide. According to the record, this is what happened: Marcus had stolen Marshall Hebert's car and was trying to run away with Louise when Bonbon accidentally caught them. Marcus started a fight and Bonbon killed him trying to protect himself. Nothing was brought up at the hearing about Marshall.

Bonbon left the plantation the day after the hearing. The night before he left, he came down to the house and tried to explain things to me. He told me he knew Marshall had put Marcus up to this—that Marcus was supposed to kill him, not him killing Marcus. But Marcus didn't have the gun that Marshall had put in the dash drawer. Bonbon told me he had seen Marshall searching in the other car after he went in the yard, but he didn't know until after the fight what Marshall was looking for. He told me he didn't want to fight Marcus, he was hoping Marcus would run from him. If Marcus had made any attempt to run, he would have let him go, and there wouldn't have been a thing said about it. But when Marcus didn't run, he had to fight him. Not just fight him, but he had to kill him. If he hadn't killed Marcus, he would have been killed himself. The Cajuns on the river would have done that.

I sat on the gallery listening to Bonbon, but I couldn't

feel any pity for him. Far as I was concerned, all the human understanding we had had between us was over with now. He saw this in my face and I could see how it hurt him. He left the house and the next day he left the plantation with his little girl. Pauline left a couple nights later with the twins. The same night of the fight, some people had taken Louise to a hospital in New Orleans. Not long after that, they took her to Jackson—the insane asylum.

The Saturday after Bonbon and Pauline left the plantation, Marshall Hebert called me to his library.

"You better leave from here," he said.

"Yes sir, I was thinking about that, myself," I said.

"These Cajuns know you and that boy lived in the same house, and they might get it in their heads to do you something."

I nodded. He wasn't worried about the Cajuns hurting me. He wanted me to leave because I knew the truth about what had happened. He was afraid I might start blackmailing now and he would have to get somebody to kill me.

Marshall was sitting behind his desk. He pushed a big envelope across the desk toward me. I picked up the envelope and took out the letter.

"It's only a recommendation," he said. "Telling people that you're a good worker."

After I had read the letter, I folded it neatly and put it back in the envelope. Then I laid the envelope on the desk.

"You don't want it?" he said, getting red in the face.

"No sir, I'll get by," I said. "Thanks very much."

I went back home and packed my things; then I went up to Aunt Margaret's house. I told her that everything I had left in the house was for her. If she couldn't use them, she could give them away.

"Sit down and eat something 'fore you leave," she said.

It was about three o'clock in the evening. I sat down at the table, and Aunt Margaret dished up a big plate of meat and rice and set it in front of me. She got a cup of coffee and sat down at the table, too.

"Yes, you have to leave," she said, nodding her head thoughtfully.

"I know," I said, eating.

"You see, you won't forget," she said.

"I can't, Aunt Margaret."

"That's why you got to go," she said. "You'll just keep reminding him."

"You forgot already, Aunt Margaret?" I asked her.

"Yes," she said.

The food was good. I ate slowly, looking across the table at her.

"When you live long as I done lived, you learn to forget things quite easy," she said.

"I can't. He killed Marcus; Bonbon didn't."

"That's what you saying," she said.

"That's what we all know," I said.

"I don't know nothing," she said, looking straight in my eyes.

"I was thinking about leaving anyhow," I said.

"Why didn't you go before now?"

I looked across the table at her. I loved Aunt Margaret very much.

"I don't know," I said.

She nodded. "I know," she said.

"But you don't know Marshall Hebert was the one who killed Marcus?"

"No, I don't know that," she said.

I ate and looked at her. "I'll be like this one day," I thought. "But Marcus never would have been like this."

279

"I wonder where they at now," she said.

"Pauline and Bonbon?"

"Yes."

"I don't know."

"You think she followed him?"

"She might have."

"They'll have to go North," Aunt Margaret said.

"That's where Marcus and Louise wanted to go," I said.

"You liked Marcus, didn't you, James?"

"At the last," I said. "Him and Louise both. They showed lot of courage."

"That's why it had to end like that," she said. "They can't let nothing like that happen now."

"Who?" I said.

"Bonbon and his kind," she said.

"But not Marshall?"

"He didn't have nothing to do with it," she said.

"Then why is he sending me away from here?" I said.

"Them Cajuns might start some mess," she said.

After I finished eating, I put my plate in the pan of soapy water on the stove. Then I came back to the table where Aunt Margaret was sitting. She stood up and I saw tears in her eyes.

"Lean down here, James," she said.

I leaned over for her. She held me close and kissed me on the jaw.

"Well, I'm going," I said.

"Where you going, James?"

"I don't know, Aunt Margaret."

We went out on the gallery. Unc Octave and Mr. Roberts were out there. Mr. Roberts had his little switch that he used for popping at flies. I told him and Unc Octave good-bye, then I hung my guitar round my neck and picked up my suitcase and handbag. Aunt Margaret followed me to the gate.

"Good-bye," I told her again.

"I'll walk piece way," she said.

She took the handbag from me. The people we met in the road told me good-bye. The ones on the galleries waved at me. Some of them inside the houses came to the door to wave at me.

When we came up to Bonbon's old house, Aunt Margaret and I stopped for a moment. The place looked cool, lonely, and very peaceful. I started shaking my head.

"I know what you mean," Aunt Margaret said.

"I was thinking about what that preacher said at Marcus's funeral," I said. " 'Man is here for a little while, then gone.' "

"Ain't it the true," Aunt Margaret said.

"Well, good-bye again," I said.

I put my hand on her shoulder and kissed her on the jaw.

"Take care yourself, James," she said.

I picked up the suitcase and the handbag and walked away. When I looked over my shoulder, I saw her going back home.

# About the Author

ERNEST J. GAINES was born on a Louisiana plantation in 1933 and spent his childhood working in the fields. At fifteen he moved to California where he completed his education and graduated from San Francisco State College in 1957. The following year he won a Wallace Stegner Creative Writing Fellowship at Stanford University. In 1959 he was awarded the Joseph Henry Jackson Award and his first novel, *Catherine Carmier,* was published in 1964. He has been widely published in various magazines and short story anthologies.